The Man God Has For You

---

*7 Traits to Help You
Determine
Your Life Partner*

STEPHAN LABOSSIERE

The Man God Has For You – 7 Traits to Help You Determine Your Life Partner

Copyright ©2018 by Stephan Speaks LLC

Published by Highly Favored Publishing

Third Edition: January 2018

For information, contact Highly Favored Publishing –
highlyfavoredent@gmail.com

Editor: ShaVaughn Morris

Formatting: Ya Ya Ya Creative – www.yayayacreative.com

ISBN No. 978-0-9980189-0-4

PRINTED AND BOUND IN THE UNITED STATES OF AMERICA

Dedication

This book is dedicated to every woman who genuinely desires true love in her life; who has ever had to deal with the struggle of dating the wrong men, or not being able to recognize the right one. I know it can get really tough, and my prayer is that every last one of you will be loved, respected, and cherished by the man who is truly best for you.

Table of Contents

Preface

I'm sure you are wondering why I wrote this book. Well, to make a long story short, God told me to. I mean that genuinely.

I don't proceed with any project unless I have prayed and asked God if I should move forward, and if this is what He wants me to do. Even before I write a chapter, I pray to make sure I say what God wants and that I provide information that can help, uplift, enlighten, and encourage you. This is not only my purpose, but also my goal with this book.

The next reason is to offer a form of guidance, from a man's perspective, on how to navigate relationships as a woman of God. You've heard on many occasions that a man is supposed to *"protect and provide"* and you may have been taught this;

however, a lot of women have not been protected and provided for. There are many woman who have not received proper *manly* guidance and advice, guidance and advice that doesn't encourage them to compromise who they are, or provide one-sided views on how men and women should operate in relationships. Advice from men who desire to see them do well; to shield and protect them from nonsense, as well as offer insight on best practices to help them navigate through life. There is security in knowing the man (or men) offering you guidance and advice has your back.

That is who I want to be for you.

I want to be the man who has your back, the guy who gives you loving guidance. The man who works to protect you mentally, emotionally, and spiritually from getting caught up in situations I know will cause more damage, and will keep you off the path where you belong.

I don't want that for you.

It is an important focal point with every book I write—each book represents pieces to a puzzle designed to make sure you get what you deserve and experience the life that God set up for you.

Also, I understand people struggle with relationships and I want to be able to breakdown every aspect. I don't believe in just writing one book and trying to mash everything into it. What you will experience are different books that cover different aspects of the puzzle, that will help you see the bigger picture. It is all created to ensure you receive what is best, as long as you embrace the information and are willing to do your part in the process.

I want to see you win.

Period.

Point blank.

I no longer want to see you hurting or lacking. I want to witness you getting everything you deserve. This is the reason why I wrote this book.

I can hear the questions now, *what about the men? The men need help too!* You are absolutely correct! I have books for men and they are available if they CHOOSE to invest. I will always be willing to encourage and help them. However, I'm going to be honest … YOU are my priority.

Women have an amazing power that is gravely important to, and in, this world. My mission to help you heal and get back on track can have such a profound impact on society. You are our mothers, sisters, and wives. Collectively, your influence is greater than you realize. Even if none of those roles apply, by being a friend, or in your day-to-day behavior; your energy is huge. I recognize its importance. I can heal one-hundred men and those hundred men may be unable to heal one woman. However, I can heal one woman and her energy has the power to impact those hundred men and more.

You may not understand or fully agree; however, I am telling you, as a man who has coached individuals for over nine years, I can attest to your capabilities as a woman and it is important to protect and nurture this, as well as assure that you are in the right place to exude this power.

That's the *why*.

Plain and simple.

Introduction

D oes God really have a man just for me? If so, where is he, when is he coming and what in the world is taking his behind so long?

I'm sure that is what you are thinking, and I understand how you feel. Waiting on the man God has for you can be annoying, frustrating, and at times, you feel hopeless. It is not an easy path to walk; however, when done right, it will without a doubt, provide the most benefit.

Does God really have a man *just* for you? Well, to be honest, the answer is yes and no.

No, because your actions can have an impact on whether you receive him or not. The idea of a "soulmate," a person you're guaranteed to be with, is simply not true. We all make decisions in life, and unfortunately many people make choices that block them from being with the person who is best for them.

Notice I said the person who is best for *them*.

This is where I believe the term "soulmate" can be applied. It is the *yes* when determining if God really has a man *just* for you. God knows the people who will walk into your life, as well as those who will align with your purpose and have successful relationships with you. He'll embrace any choice you make, but what you believe is a good choice may not be God's idea of a good choice. Many of you are familiar with the phrase "wait for your Boaz." For those who are not familiar, here is a quick explanation.

Boaz is a biblical character from the Book of Ruth who becomes Ruth's husband. Part of her story speaks to her experience of receiving a good man and is often used as reference for single women who hope to one day marry. The phrase itself is symbolic of saying, *wait on the man God has for you*. Ruth's story shows proof that when you move forward in obedience, patience, and faith, you can receive the blessings that await you.

So again, does God have a man who is *just* for you?

Well, to be technical, if you read 1 Corinthians 11:9 KJV, it states,

> *Neither was the man created for the woman; but the woman for the man.*

Basically, you were created to be a blessing to a man who puts God first. Not that this is your only purpose, but with regard to relationships, this is the dynamic. Ultimately, you have to be able to recognize who is worthy of you as their blessing and who is your best fit. What I am going to discuss in this book will help you to recognize the qualities that need to be in place before you move forward with a man of interest. You will also get a glimpse into the work that must be done on your end, for him to receive you.

As you continue to read through this guide, I want you to pray about what you read. I don't expect you to take my word as bond simply because I am Stephan "the relationship coach," or Stephan who has all these "followers" on social media—no. I want you to accept what I say because you've gone to God, you've asked him about it, and He has given you the green light. This is not specific to this book, it is for everything. Even when the pastor tells you something, or when someone comes into your life and prophesies over you, or the friend that offers you advice, or anyone who gives you information, go back to God and verify. Be sure that the information is for you. Don't just walk away with a person's word or guidance. People are not God.

I am not God.

I am the messenger, the middle man; however, there are still a lot of people who scream and claim that they are messengers for God. They claim to have your best interest in mind, when in truth, they are setting you up for disaster. I can say with confidence, that is not my purpose. I would be a hypocrite to say, "Don't pray about what I say, but you *should* pray about what everyone else says."

No.

Pray about it all.

Pray about everything you consider implementing in your life.

Prayer is not only important to ensure you receive the right information, but it also helps you to cultivate and nurture your relationship with God. To develop the habit of talking to and hearing from Him is key. You must learn to hear Him more than anyone or anything else.

Lastly, be open and receptive to what you read. Some of it may be a refresher, while some may be new and eye-opening. There are nuggets in here that will really hit you, but you have to be willing to accept and implement the new strategies in your life. Don't read this book and continue as you were, holding on to the same perceptions. Be open to explore a different approach. Now don't get me wrong, if all is well and perfect in your life, then by all means, proceed as you are; however, I am sure that is not the case and I believe that is a fair assumption.

With that said, don't be afraid.

Much of what you read may open the door to vulnerability, and that is a good thing. It will be scary and a hard pill to swallow, but it is in your best interest and that is what matters.

In this book, you'll find not just the *7 Traits*, but also additional topics I've included throughout the text as supplements. These supplements go a bit more in depth regarding topics I have discussed with my followers on social media, other clients, people at events, and in casual conversations. I'll dispel one of the biggest myths in dating, breakdown the most common perception shared among friends, family and the internet, as well as help you shift how you communicate with God.

I'm grateful you have chosen to walk this journey with me and I hope you are ready to get into the next chapter.

Myth

Myth

There Aren't Enough Men for Every Woman to Receive Her "Boaz"

Since writing *God, Where is My Boaz*, I've gotten detractors.

People who love to spread this false belief that there aren't enough men for every woman, that every woman won't find their mate. Based on this belief, these detractors claim my message is a dream, a fairy tale, or an unattainable goal for a lot of women, that it sets them up for failure. This doesn't just apply to people on social media and the gurus, it is also those you value; pastors, spiritual coaches, even your friends and family share these false narratives and it makes me sick. It is a message of sabotage that kills the hope, faith, and belief of a woman who patiently awaits and prepares to receive a loving relationship in her life. It promotes the idea to give up and let go, and they insist they are being more *real* and *honest* with this negativity. It is ridiculous, and bottom line is that they are dead wrong. I am a firm believer that you will receive the man God has for you.

Plain and simple.

Here's an analogy …

Imagine there is a club called *You Get a Man*. Better yet, it is called *You Get a **Husband***, because you are not just looking for a man. Your desire is to receive a husband, a partner with whom you will share your life. So, we have the club *You Get a Husband*, and in line are women from all backgrounds and beliefs. As a woman of God, you have VIP status and access. With this access, you get to skip the line since God gives His people the best. As long as you do what is necessary to get on the VIP list, you don't have to wait with the crowd.

But here is what happens.

You go to the front of the line, security asks you for ID and you don't have it.

I'm not talking about your license or passport. Not that ID. I am referring to your *internal* ID, the one that wakes up with you, the one you see in the mirror each day, the one people recognize as soon as you walk in the door—that ID.

Why would you **not** have that ID?

It is because you have not yet discovered who you are. You have not become the person God designed you to be, you have not walked in your purpose. You have not quite figured out your life. Although you have VIP access and can go to the front of the line, you can't get in because you are not prepared. You haven't done the work to receive all God has in store for you.

Be clear, this is not to discourage you. There is no point in worrying about statistics about how many men there are or what you won't have.

The point is, you get to skip the line.

You are set apart from the rest because you have VIP access, but do you know who you are?

Before you get concerned with the amount of men there are in the world, and whether or not you will get one, you have to be right with YOU and

God. You have to discover your greatest self and there are three keys to accomplishing this.

#1 – Heal From Your Past

One of the core components to discovering who you are, is to heal from your past. When you heal from your past, you are able to become right with yourself and with God. When you have not healed from your past, no matter how much you want love or think you are ready for it, there will be a struggle. Not healing from your past prevents you from moving forward and when love comes your way, you will run. Of course, it sounds crazy to run from love and not take advantage of it when it comes your way; however, when you haven't let go of past hurt and pain, it blocks you from being vulnerable. Vulnerability is necessary for you to not just receive love, but also give it. It is the bridge that assists with nurturing the type of relationship God wants for you. Lack of healing will prevent you from accepting that love.

When you haven't healed, it blinds you. Ladies, hurt and pain blinds you. If you have never acknowledged or properly resolved your past issues, when you attempt to navigate through life, it will be as if you are walking through your house in the dark, or down the street with broken glasses on. You can't see straight! This skewed vision or lack of foresight causes you to end up with the wrong person, in a bad relationship, or holding on to situations way longer than you should. Being blind to nonsense is detrimental to your spiritual and emotional sanctity.

Lastly, not healing from your past stops you from exuding positive energy. Positive energy is necessary to attract the great relationship you seek. Let's be honest here, although you may be a good or a great woman it doesn't mean you are a positive one. If you are not positive, you will struggle to attract and embrace the right man. You will attract men who only want sex and will waste your time with no problem. Those guys don't care about your negative energy. Their only concern is how you look, what they can get out of you, and how they can take advantage of you.

For the man who genuinely seeks a true relationship, seeing or sensing negative energy will push him away and turn him off. Or he will assume he is a bother, not welcomed in your presence, and will walk away. It is imperative that you do what is necessary to get the healing you need in order to embrace the love that is for you.

#2 – Finding Your Purpose

I know a lot of this sounds easier said than done; however, it still needs to happen. If you don't know where you are going, you won't know who belongs with you on that path. Aside from that, you won't find your true happiness.

In the previous section I discussed how being positive, exuding that energy and healing yourself, is essential; however, what contributes to this is being happy. You have to do things you enjoy and find a career that speaks to your heart in order to radiate this great energy. You have to appreciate where you are. Although the process of getting there may be a struggle, there is a sense of peace that comes from within when you are confident you are walking the path God is leading you on. The comfort of knowing who you are and what you are meant to do is essential. You don't want to end up in a relationship and realize the man you are with doesn't cosign, feel comfortable, or agree with the path God has for you.

That strain will set you back and keep you from fully embracing who you are.

There are plenty of women, right now, who are not walking in their purpose because they are trying to walk with the wrong man and he is holding them back. He becomes an anchor in their life. They are stuck, unable to progress the way God intended.

And it is not just the men.

The wrong friends, other negative associations in your life, your job, a myriad of things that don't belong can represent the anchor. In order for you to know what fits, you must know where you are supposed to go. It is important that you to take the time to make sense of your purpose.

#3 – Know How to Hear God

A lot of women tell me that they pray but after further conversation, I notice they are not listening. As you move forward in the book, I'll address this more in detail.

What is your intent when you enter prayer? Do you pray to make a request, or to vent? Do you pray in a moment of distress, or to ask a question and receive an answer? I get that this is not easy for everyone. There is so much to learn in regards to praying properly and knowing how to hear God. It is important you get to a point where you enter prayer with the intent to listen to what God says, because that is how you will receive directions.

Mutually, men and women are supposed to be obedient to God; however, this cannot happen without knowledge of the orders or directions. We all have specific instructions. Sure, the Bible, spiritual leaders, and even I aid you on your journey giving you guidance; however, to get down to the crux of what you are supposed to do, that guidance needs to be specific and from God. There will be instances where you are told to go left while someone else has to go right, and you will need more than just the scripture and service alone. These tools are in place to complement God's message in prayer, and confirm what you have been told.

As I said earlier, with everything, including this book, go back and confirm with God that this is the correct information for your life. If you hear anything different, go with that. What God says trumps anything I have to say, anything your pastor, friends, or family say, and even what you *want* to do. We struggle with hearing God because we don't like the message. We don't like (or approve) of the path He has told us to walk. It doesn't make sense or add up. But, to have what is best we have to listen, then act.

Me writing this book is listening, then being obedient.

This is why I am here, doing this, speaking to you, trying to help. I am doing my best to be obedient and do what is required of me. My prayer is that this will help you, so ultimately I want you to do the same for your life, because that is what will help you.

✳ ✳ ✳ ✳

God is not bound by numbers.

I live in Atlanta which is notorious for its perceived lopsided male to female ratio. When the numbers are lumped together, there's only a 3.0% difference between the number of men and women in the city; however, what alarms most women is the number of SINGLE women that outnumber the amount of single and available men. This lack of availability may be due to various reasons such as sexual preference, incarceration, and other statuses that knock men off the list; however, this also applies to women. As lopsided as the numbers may appear, they really aren't what they're assumed to be. Still, this does not matter.

Think about it.

You are working with God and have faith He can provide you with everything, a life filled with abundance, but you think He will shortchange you on a man? There is enough for everything else, but not enough men? You honestly believe that is how it works?

No, it does not.

Remember, you are at the front of the line, you are a VIP. You get to skip ahead of everyone else, but you have to do your part to be ready when the doors open. Be honest with yourself. Be honest about not doing the things you need to be doing. Even if you think you have done all you need to, there may be things you overlooked. Again, it is not to pass judgement, discourage you, or make you feel saddened in any way. It is to help you understand there are pieces to the puzzle that you can add which will bring the results you are looking for.

Always know there is work to be done on your end.

Be open to making improvements and adjustments. Be confident that these steps can get you results. Don't get distracted by those who claim they are doing their thing with no results. When you start to speak to people on a deeper level, you will discover what has been overlooked, skipped, and not addressed. This is why the puzzle pieces don't fall into place for a lot of people.

When you are ready to change and receive what God has for you, do the work. Never believe there is not enough for you. There is an abundance for those who follow and trust God in everything. There are no limitations. Do your part, stay the course, remain positive, and everything will be yours.

Trait #1

Trait #1

You Will Be Attracted to Him

*Y*ou *know what they say, God don't like ugly …* OK, so the phrase refers to a person's behavior, not their looks; however, it is a suitable quote for what we are about to discuss.

Believers are oftentimes encouraged to accept that looks should not matter or be as important as other factors, instead to focus on the inside, because that is what counts. I agree. Looks should not be the focal point when seeking a partner; however, they should not be ignored. God isn't trying to set you up with someone you are not attracted to.

Think about it.

Why would God want this? It is an important piece of a romantic relationship. It is the reality of how things are; yet, attraction becomes the excuse people use when they want you to settle or accept less. They'll claim you're being "too picky" and because they want you to rush to be with someone, they will encourage you to overlook a lack of attraction.

For instance, if a person doesn't want their looks used against them, they will downplay the importance to avoid hurting their chances of being with you. Family members and friends will dismiss it because they want to connect you with someone they know may not be the most attractive in your eyes. None of this means looks are not important, or that you should buy into the idea that God wants you to be with someone you are not attracted to.

Looks vs. Attraction

There is a difference between *looks* and *attraction*. This is where I believe a lot of people get confused. When saying *looks shouldn't be important*, it is the specifics about a person's physical attributes that you need to avoid. I do not believe you should have a list. If the requirements include this man being six feet tall, with a specific hair and eye color, and a particular build, then yes, that should not be so important. The package in which God will send the person He has for you may not be what you expect, but the person will have everything you need and attraction will be part of it.

So what is the difference?

When two people have an attraction, it is specific to the action or power of sparking an interest, pleasure, or the like for someone or something. It is the force that draws a connection, which I will get to later on in the book.

There are different types of attraction. You can attract, or be attracted, to someone in many ways. Physical attraction is important, and although this attributes to sexual attraction, what you ultimately want is to develop a romantic attraction with someone. This particular attraction brings the desire of a romantic relationship and determines if this person is for you.

We all have our preferences, desires, and physical traits that we are drawn to, and still found ourselves attracted to someone who does not fit our particular style. It is the attraction that is important, not if the world thinks they are cute, or if your friends think they are hot. The attraction is there despite them not having your preferred look, and if it is not, I would never tell you to move forward. Doing so is detrimental and I'll provide the reasons why; however, if the attraction is in place, even if they are not your typical style, you should be open to it and embrace it.

Attraction is the ingredient that transitions a relationship from platonic to romantic. Without it, you have friendship, roommates, "play cousins," anything but a romantic relationship.

There is no way around it.

To expect you, or anyone, to enter a romantic relationship with someone where there is no attraction would be foolish and lead to bigger problems than you can imagine.

Many of you may clap your hands in agreement, happy that someone finally confirmed what you have known all along. People tried to convince you otherwise, told you it is not a big deal and to ignore it. Even beaten you down with the idea and encouraged you to settle for someone less attractive. On the other hand, some of you may wonder what real issue would it cause. You believe you can grow to like this person, the attraction to him being the least of your worries. If you have entertained the thought of moving forward with someone you are not attracted to, I need you to understand why this a HUGE problem. I'll share three key reasons.

#1 – Lack of Effort

When there is a lack of attraction, there is a lack of effort. Whether you admit it or not, when you are not drawn to or physically desire a person, your effort in the relationship suffers. In fact, you will expect them to give more. In your mind, they are not cute enough for you to do all this extra stuff. And you may not say it out loud, but those subconscious thoughts will show in your behavior. You will react with disapproval and dismiss him without thought. The lack of attraction brings less motivation and drive to put in the work and effort. You will believe they should work harder to keep you.

You may think having the upper hand is not all that bad, still, if you are not prepared, or lack the desire to put in the effort, you will never get the results you are looking for in a relationship. You will be unfulfilled because you have not fulfilled your partner. They may pick up the slack because of their initial infatuation. Eventually this will become burdensome for them and eventually, they will crumble. The lack of desire and attraction leads to a lack of effort.

If you need further proof, look at those who are married.

Attraction has become this taboo topic that does not get discussed. It is not talked about the way it should, and we love to mask its necessity. We believe that *if we love the person, then attraction shouldn't matter*. However, when you pay attention to married couples and notice the "flame" fizzing out, or the lack of effort and desire, I guarantee that in many cases, you will find that the attraction has dwindled. The drop in attraction could be due to many reasons such as physical changes, lack of trust or betrayal; however, something occurred which impacted the ability for that person to remain attracted to their partner. One way or another, it is not the same. There is a direct correlation between a lack of attraction and a lack of effort.

Plain and simple.

#2 – Lack of Affection

I have witnessed couples where the woman barely wants to be touched by the man. She will try to mask it with phrases such as, *I'm just not an affectionate person or I'm not in the mood*, when the real truth is that the attraction to her partner is not strong enough, and she does not want *him* touching her like that. Bring the right man along and it is a completely different story. Their affection towards their children, friends, and other people is evident, but not with their own man. Sure, there are other issues that lead to lack of affection, but what I am telling you here, in this chapter, is that a lack of attraction will impact and create a lack of affection.

Do not even think about fighting me on this one and NO, you CANNOT get passed it!

If you are not giving your partner affection, they will not feel desired in the relationship, and if they feel undesired, it is going to cause problems. It will affect their ability to compromise. It will affect how they feel, as well as create negative energy. And I know you do not want to hear (or believe) this, but yes, it opens the door to infidelity. When a person is not feeling desired at home, I guarantee, someone is going to come along and give them what they need outside the home. It is a natural gravitation because as people, we like to feel desired. Affection is simply an extension and expression of that desire, so when it is removed, it leaves a void to be filled.

#3 – Lack of Respect

This goes back to what I mentioned previously about a man not being "cute enough" for you to work this hard. When there is not enough attraction, it is very easy for a lack of respect to show up, and if you pay attention to most couples, you will see it more often than not. The obvious is that a lack of respect will destroy a relationship.

There is no way around it.

You might think you can work around it. That you would not stoop to those levels, or entertain such things; however, it is very easy to believe that in the beginning. You have to consider the long-term effects when you ignore things like attraction and other red flags I'll discuss further along in the book. You have to understand that you are setting yourself up for failure and be honest about your ability to work past this while you two are together.

It is my hope that the plan is be with them for the rest of your life, so can you really handle that? Can you really handle a lack of attraction with your partner for the rest of your life? They are not going to wake up one day and be "cute" to you. You are not going to wake up one day and all of a sudden want them NOW more than ever. It is not impossible, because people go to a lot of drastic measures or make certain changes that can affect attraction; however, you cannot go in expecting that to happen, and in most cases, it does not.

The lack of attraction should not be ignored.

Still, I can hear some of you saying, *but looks fade, looks go away. Why should we be so concerned with attraction and looks?* Again, looks are only physical, while attraction refers to the interest and the like of the entire package, not just the parts.

Older couples are perfect examples.

Even though their looks may have faded as society sees it, when they see each other they still recognize the subtleties and nuances that made them beautiful to each other. That is what fueled the attraction to their partner. Know that there is a difference between aging, letting yourself go, and not being attracted to someone from the beginning.

Saying looks fade is not an excuse to overlook it.

Money comes and goes, are you going around looking for a broke man right now? Health fades, are you going to the ER to find a date? No! You are not doing any of that, so don't give me this "looks fade" stuff. The issue is still impactful to your situation. It does not go away or allow itself to be overlooked with the belief you will still be able to have this happy, glorious, wonderful relationship, regardless of its absence. You cannot be in denial about that. You cannot run away from that truth. You have to be honest with yourself about what you can handle and not try to ignore it simply to appease other people wanting you in a relationship. Or you feel your clock ticking and rush into a relationship with a man who is mediocre or "safe," because you don't believe you have time to wait for the "right" guy.

Or …

You don't trust being with someone you are overly attracted to, or the guy you consider "too good looking." I can't tell you how many women I come across who fear being with a really good looking guy.

For just as many women who love being with a man other women desire, there are just as many who fear it. It is clear there is a deeper issue that needs to be addressed and not simply think the solution is, "let me get with a guy who just doesn't look that good."

It is OK if the guy doesn't fit the profile you would have desired if you made your own list; however, if you are not genuinely attracted to him, you should not move forward. Know that this is not who God sent for you. He wants your relationship to glorify Him. How does this happen if there is a lack of affection, respect, effort, and desire?

This does not reflect well upon God.

It makes people believe what He has brought together look bad. No one will want any of it, especially if you claim God had His hand on it. Trust and believe that every relationship that consists of two people who have gone to God, talked to Him and made sure that they were supposed to be together, is to glorify Him. Be an example of the greatness God can provide.

Yes, it may come in an unexpected package, and not fit the dynamic or the qualifications other people think you should shoot for; however, what will speak loudest is your joy, happiness, positive energy, and desire for your partner. That should be there and attraction is a big part of it.

While attraction is important at the beginning stages, it is even more important once you are further along in your relationship. Understand that if you love your partner, if you care about them, you will want to do things to feed, maintain, and nurture the attraction. You cannot get into the mindset of *they should just accept me for me, love me anyway*—no. If you love them, you should want to look good for them. This goes for men and women. In any romantic relationship, regardless of what it is, if you are trying to be together in the long run, then you want to embrace that.

That is a future note, put a pin in it for when the time comes.

For now, remember that you will be attracted to the man God has for you. If that does not exist, don't think you are expected to move forward. Always remember to pray and ask God. Make sure this is the man that He wants you to move forward with, so that you can go forth in peace and not with an unsettled feeling of getting less than what you desire, or what makes you happy. That is not what God wants for your life or for your relationship.

Trait #2

Trait #2

His Love Will Cherish You, Not Disrespect You

I know what you are thinking …

This should be obvious, common sense. Unfortunately, common sense is not always so common. The fact is that a lot of people, possibly even you, are experiencing abusive and/or toxic relationships, relationships with men who exhibit negative and disrespectful behavior. Even if you are not currently in this situation, you could be the person that believes you would never put up with this type of behavior. It is unacceptable and it would never happen to you. Then in the blink of an eye, you are in it and do not know how to get out. It is now a situation you find yourself struggling with for various reasons. It could be a reflection of your upbringing or other relationships you have experienced. You may believe it is not as bad as it appears. However, the fact remains, you have to be aware that any man who continues to disrespect or mistreat you is not a man sent from God.

Here is why you may not fully understand the issue.

It is possible you were raised in a dysfunctional home. A lot of people have been around negative, unhealthy, toxic behavior and, to some extent, tried to normalize it. They paint the picture as "*this is just what happens in relationships.*" When this environment is normalized, you do not realize or grasp how unhealthy it is. You begin to validate, rationalize, explain and sweep it under the rug. What is evident is that it is a problem and should not be dismissed.

Another reason you may not grasp the issue is the lack of healthy and happy examples of relationships. The lack of examples makes your relationship appear as if it is not any worse than what the people around you experience. Therefore, you believe you are better off and it makes you blind to what is occurring. Not to mention that these issues more than likely started way before you got into the relationship. Although some of you may not be with anyone currently, you have to make note of the red flags. Oftentimes, some women paint certain jealous or possessive behaviors as acts of love.

I will never forget my former client.

She was a mother who tried to justify the actions of her stalker boyfriend. This man parked outside the house and watched her every move. She had convinced herself that this is what people do when they are in love.

Really!

This is a mother justifying toxic behavior so, of course, when the daughter is older, she will struggle with understanding why this is wrong, as well as when to draw the line in a similar situation. I am certain this woman's past includes relationships even more toxic than this, so to her, it was nothing. It was no big deal. She will sweep it under the rug and continue to validate it. She will make it seem as if it is all good because she's speaking from a place of brokenness, where she hasn't healed, which is the next reason why you may not grasp the issue.

You will notice *healing from your past* is a repeated foundation of not only accepting love, but also being able to recognize the man God has for you. Of all I mentioned, your friends and the unhealthy household, if you have not healed from what you have been exposed to or witnessed, that brokenness you are holding on to will prevent you from recognizing the toxic relationship or person you are dealing with. It will prevent you from breaking free. Subconsciously, you will always find reasons to remain in a situation where you do not belong.

I acknowledge there may be some bickering, arguments, and even a moment where a disrespectful act occurs. Every situation won't be a recurring issue, just as every man isn't going to be toxic. Certain issues can be handled effectively and resolved. In order to understand this, you have to know the difference between a mistake and a real issue. between a *mistake* and a *real issue*.

A **mistake** happens once with the issue being acknowledged. Even if it happened twice, it is unlikely for the two incidents to occur in a short span of time and still be regarded as a mistake. I will give you an example.

Let's use the woman from the scenario above. Let's say the woman said something disrespectful to her boyfriend in the heat of an argument. He let her know how this affects him, how it makes him feel. She apologizes, recognizes that it is an issue; however, somewhere down the line, she gets upset and does it again. It is possible for the second time to be a mistake because she may have lost her composure and it happened, still, she is genuinely trying to work on it and has shown an effort.

This same principle can apply to a man.

It is possible he did it once and it was a mistake. He acknowledged it, he has worked on it, you saw progress, he had a moment, but he is back on track. Notice I said: **he acknowledged it**. If a person does not acknowledge what they did, if they do not take ownership of it, then you are not dealing with a mistake—it is a **real issue**. It is a much bigger problem because nothing can be fixed if that person sees no wrong in what they did, if they continually defend, validate or excuse it. It is a clear indication that it will, without a doubt, happen again.

If you tell a person what you dislike, and all the person does is make excuses about how you pushed them to that point, or claim they did it because "that is just how they are," it is going to happen again because they do not see the problem.

There Has to be Genuine Progress

Genuine progress is determined by recognizing the conscious effort. We know when someone is putting forth the effort to ensure they respond differently and take a better path of resolution in those situations. If there is no effort to make better choices or walk a better path, then it is not a mistake but a *real issue*.

It is one thing to say, "oh, I'm sorry, my bad, I won't do it again," because I know that you are upset and it is an issue I just want to get under control. However, that does not mean I understand what I did. If I don't understand how throwing your past in your face makes you upset and feel insecure in the relationship, I am going to have a hard time not committing the same violation. When there is no connection to the problem, there is a greater chance to commit the same infraction. It is human nature.

You want to make sure there is a level of understanding, and granted some people may not completely connect, but at the very least, they need to recognize that it affects you and that it is a problem. It is even better when they can understand *why* it is a problem, *why* it affects you, *why* it is an issue. Then, it will give them more fuel and a greater ability to avoid committing the same offense.

So again, in order to qualify someone's actions as a mistake, they have to first be *willing to acknowledge the issue and own it*, they have to *show genuine progress* in trying to do things better, and lastly, they need to *understand the issue*. It is only when these three things take place that an action can be labeled a mistake. This justifies the reasons it can be resolved and how you can still move forward with this person. If those requirements are not met, the action is not a mistake. It is a real issue and that is not the man God has for you or he simply isn't ready.

To be clear, the man God has for you is not going to be the perfect in that he will never do anything wrong. We all slip up. We are human beings. We sin, we do bad things sometimes—that is life. Still, there is a difference between the person who makes a mistake, and wants to do better and be better for you, as opposed to the person who does it and does not care about how you feel. They do not give one damn about how this affects you. All they care about is themselves, how they feel, and what they are looking to get out of a situation.

A person like that will always dismiss your feelings and the impact of their actions. It will not matter if they use the household excuse or claim *it's just the way I am*, they need to seek counseling. They need to get help. When they have healed and corrected their issues, only then can that person come back, or you can consider the possibility of them coming back. You are not obligated to remain with someone while they continue to behave in a toxic manner. They need to be actively trying to correct it, and to be clear, active does not mean they continue the actions while claiming to be making the corrections. There has to be visible change.

The red flags cannot be ignored.

It does not get better later in the relationship. It does not get better once you marry the person, nor does it magically stop. The more you continue to pacify the behavior and dismiss the problem, the more you enable them. You tell them their actions are OK. It does not matter what you say, how much you yell, scream, kick, or hit, if you continue to entertain it and not address the issue, and in some cases, end the relationship only to take them right back, then you're saying to them, **this is acceptable**.

It is not. It is a problem.

Although we are referring to a man's behavior, sometimes it could be you. You may be the abusive or toxic one. You may be the one that is engaging in disrespectful behavior, not owning up to it and validating it with how you were raised, what you were exposed to, or simply because you are mad and should have the right to act on it in a particular way. If this is you, then you need to seek the counseling.

There is not enough encouragement for people to seek counseling.

Seeking counseling or third party, unbiased assistance is good for you. It is healthy. We all need a greater state of emotional health and we gain that by being able to process what we have been through, how we are feeling, as well as work through the issues we have ignored throughout our lives. Whether we want to acknowledge it or not, it is impacting our physical, mental, and, emotional health. Addressing these issues is important, so if you see a problem encourage counseling. What will aid in getting the man to consider counseling is being able to say you did it yourself. No one likes to be singled out, told they are the issue, or told *you need go to counseling, but I never went because I don't have any problems*.

That is not how this works.

I have gone to counseling. As a coach, I had to make sure I did my healing so that I could then suggest it to you and encourage you from a positive and healthy place. We can all use it, so do not be afraid to not just suggest it, but go yourself.

Be sure you are not the one creating the problem and setting the stage for these toxic battles and behaviors. Again, none of this validates their actions, or them being toxic. I do not want you to excuse disrespectful behavior because of what you did. However, I want you to be mindful of whether you are creating, or contributing to the situation and understand that correcting your behavior first is priority. You have to fix what you are doing before you can focus on anyone else.

You are God's daughter.

Just as any father wants the best for his daughter, God wants the best for you. He does not want you in unhealthy and toxic relationships. He is not trying to set you up with any man who is going to be consistently disrespectful to you or mistreat you. That's not the case and it is never normal. I understand what you saw, or what your friends accept in their lives. I understand the impact of who your mother, or whomever dealt with; Regardless it is unacceptable and you shouldn't expose yourself to it.

If you or a friend are in, or ever find yourself in, an abusive relationship, I want to share the number for the National Domestic Abuse Hotline. I think it is important for everyone to know who they can reach out to for assistance if the situation arises. I know sometimes it is difficult to pull yourself out once you are in, and it is even more difficult to know who you can trust when you may not be able to go to your family and friends.

The number to the National Domestic Abuse Hotline is:

1-800-799-7233

To be clear, I do not have any business partnerships, nor did they pay me to mention them. I am telling you this because it is a valuable resource and oftentimes, we do not know these resources exist. I want to make sure you have it.

As God's daughter, as His child, He wants the best for you. Disrespect and mistreatment do not belong there because that does not glorify God. It does not speak to the greatness He wants to provide you and is not an example of what He is setting up for your life. Always be aware of this and when it is contrary to His blessings, remove it. Remove it and move on because there is something greater waiting around the corner.

Trait #3

Trait #3

You Will Not Have to Make Him Into a Man

I hear a lot of rhetoric about building a man.

Being able to grow with him and be patient during his process, willing to be with him at his lowest point, so on and so forth, blah, blah, blah. That is not to be disrespectful; however, I know without a doubt that this is pointing a lot of women in the wrong direction, and it might be you.

Listen …

God did not make you to be a man's crutch. You are not designed to carry a man. Yes, I do believe in the idea of being supportive, being an inspiration and motivation for a man, to encourage and help him grow. However, it should all be done as his friend—genuine friends. Not giving up the booty friends, not "friends with girlfriend benefits" friends; I am talking *friend* friends. Boundaries need to be in place because God did not set you up with a boy in order for you to make him into a man.

That is incorrect.

There are consequences that come with this approach and people blindly encourage others to walk into these situations without explaining what they are. The real issue is that it sounds great on the surface. You are a "ride or die," always there for him. You will take him even when he is broke. It sounds good, but it is not an effective approach. I am not saying it has not worked for some, but more often than not, it will not work. In the next few pages, I have outlined why you should not date a man's potential and why there are a lot of risks associated in doing so.

#1 – He May Never Reach His Potential With You

When people apply themselves, they are capable of, and can accomplish, amazing things in their lives. The problem is, what you see in him may not be accurate, or it may simply be a reflection of his capabilities. This does not mean he connects with what you see in him.

Regardless of what you desire out of a man, what you think or fantasize about who and what he can be, he may not connect with that vision. If it does not connect, chances are you will drag him there and he will kick and scream along the way. When you do that, you become resentful and lose some respect for him. Dating his potential is risky because if he does not walk the path you expect or desire, it is going to stir up a lot of negative energy in the relationship.

You have to be willing to accept that this person is who they show you. Do not get me wrong, I believe there are instances where if a man shows you his vision, shows you effort, shows that he is putting in work, that is "potential" you can grasp. Although, that is not his potential you are dating at that moment, it is his character. His character shows you a man of value, someone you can respect and trust, as well as believe they will get to a better destination. Many of you may have overlooked character. You held on to the perception you want to believe he can achieve.

That is the wrong way to go.

Let him show you who he is and if it does not meet the standard you need in your life right now, move on. Even if you think, by some magical chance, he can get there, now is not the time to be with him. At the very least, you are still better off being his friend and not his "play girlfriend."

#2 – Supporting a Man vs. Sponsoring a Man

The next reason why it is wrong for you to try to build a man, and essentially carry him on your back, is the confusion with *supporting* a man versus *sponsoring* one.

The problem is that your investment in him can create an unhealthy attachment. I am sure you have experienced situations, where you felt as if you poured into him in some way. Maybe you gave yourself sexually, encouraged him, or helped him. You may have even given him money, paid bills, offered favors, or whatever it was at the time. When you believe you have made this investment, you want a return. Now, you have become blinded trying to validate the work you put in, the time and the effort spent. You have lost sight of the fact that he is not giving you what you need. You are unhappy and this relationship is not moving in the direction you desire and deserve.

Be mindful of where you place your investment.

Stocks can gain or lose value and the investor has to know when to buy or sell. It is the same when investing in relationships. If you see it is not working, you have to be able to walk away and accept that maybe you purchased bad stock.

That is the downfall of dating potential, as well as the downfall of trying to build a man. It is not easy to let go. The best route is not to bother with someone who will not match your effort. You have to be prepared to do these things without feeling as if you have lost when you don't get your desired result. It is best to do this in the mode of being a friend. You will see more of the theme of friendship throughout this chapter.

Being his friend is easier than *investing*. When you invest, it falls under the dynamic of a romantic relationship. In that instance, your investment goes far beyond the money and the time. It is your emotional energy, the fantasy of what you are hoping things will be. It is not to say this cannot happen in friendship;

however, there is a barrier, a boundary set that keeps you at bay to a certain extent. If at any point you feel as if you are becoming too attached, or caught up while friends, then it is no longer appropriate. It is not safe because you are expecting something in return you may never get. The man you befriend has to work with you, you cannot be working for him.

I will go even further with an analogy.

Let's say you and this person decide to build a house together. You show up at the site with the tools and materials, while he comes through with a drink, a sandwich, and his lawn chair, then sits there and watches you do the work. This is happening in so many situations. He is sitting back and you are doing the work.

That is not **building** with someone.

Building with someone means you and that person equally bring something to the table. They match your effort. When the dynamic is that you are more well-off than he is, there is no reason for him not to pick up the slack in other areas, while you two are "building" together. He should contribute to the relationship equally. This does not mean you have to call each other a certain amount of times per day, or spend this amount of money on each other, that is not the case. It means you are fulfilled from him, just as he is fulfilled from you. If you are not content where things are in the relationship, that is not where you need to be.

#3 – Don't Neglect Yourself

The third and key reason why you should not build a man is that *you stop building yourself*. You become so focused on this man and the energy you are putting into him that you forget about you. You believe that you are good and you have it all together, but you do not.

Not sorry.

I have to be honest with you, there is still room for improvement. There are still some things you need to learn. Even entertaining a situation like this indicates corrections that need to be made, along with the healing and growth that needs to occur. While you are busy pouring into this man, what are you pouring into you and are you still connecting with God?

We often become consumed with the person we want to be with, to the point of not realizing we have put them above God. We are worshipping them more than God, we are doing for them, trying to spend more time with them, focused and worried about their opinion more than God's. It is a setup for disaster and definitely not the relationship God wants for you.

I will not rule out the possibility that he can change. I have seen situations where men pulled themselves together; however, it is not likely when the woman is carrying them. The women stepped back, gave them space to get it together, and reconnected when they were ready. It is in those situations that, if he is serious, if he really wants it, he will quickly tighten up. Watch how quickly he wants to get back on the right track. Even if it takes him time, when he reaches the point that he is serious about being with you, he will start to clean up his act. But this does not happen when you are holding and carrying him.

#4 – Don't Enable His Laziness

You enable his procrastination, his lack of ambition, the unwillingness to do more in life and provide more for you because you are accepting it. It is hidden under the guise of support and "building with him."

No, those are lies.

He is using you, training you, and damaging you in the process. That is not where you belong. If he genuinely cares, then he needs to respect that you have to step back because the situation is not healthy. Once again, this is not where God wants you to be. He is not going to place you in unhealthy attachments, where you invest into men who may not ever even live up to the hope. Even worse is that you invest in this man, then he moves on to someone else.

Now you are super salty, or in other words, vexed.

You did all this work only for him to go give the benefits of his growth to someone else. That fear and concern contributes to the attachment and struggle with your inability to let go. The aftermath, if he does move on, is that you are frustrated, bitter, and hurt all because you were pouring into a man who was not for you.

Consider this, a lot of men will date up, so when he is in a struggle period, he has no problem trying to latch on to a woman doing better who will carry him. Him dating up, or dating you at that moment, might be because you are a meal ticket, which is why when he finally gets himself together, he moves on to someone else. When he is at that level, his mindset is different. He is not dating you at his best, he is dating you at his worst and that makes you a "come up." It sounds harsh and may hurt to hear if you are in this type of situation, but I have to be honest. I cannot lie to you. Although this may not be every instance, it is the situation in many cases.

You want him to want and desire you at *his* best. Not best specific to finances and career, but *best* with regard to his character. A man who is a hard worker and does his thing. A man willing to pour into you just as much as they hope you pour into them. A man who wants you happy just as you desire their happiness. This is who you want to date. When these things are not in place, you are dealing with a boy who you are trying to make into a man.

Again, if you want to encourage and support a man who is not quite there yet, do it as a friend. Give yourself an opportunity to see if there is a genuine connection, which I will expound more on that later in the book. You want to ensure that you have something substantial that is deeper than what you can do for him. You want to avoid being someone who is constantly giving and not getting anything in return. Be careful about crossing romantic lines with a man who is not at a level you need, or one you can be happy with now.

I hope the reasons presented here are clear as to why you should not build a man. The exception to this rule is effort you can see, tangible results. There is a difference between the guy who puts in the hours and time when he gets laid-off to find a new job, as opposed to the guy who sits on the couch while you job search and put in applications for him. Trust me, that happens and it has happened to some of you.

These are the situations I want you to avoid.

Do not entertain, defend, or allow someone to convince you it is OK, and call it support. You are not his crutch. Support his effort in doing his part in the relationship. If this is not visible, you do not need to be there.

Plain and simple.

Be focused and mindful of the signs. Do not be guilted into feeling as if you have to embrace a man at a stage that is not truly best for you. You deserve the best and if he is serious about being with you, then he will step up his game.

Reminder

Reminder

Do Not Settle

D o not settle.

Know and embrace your worth.

Do not entertain any man's nonsense.

These are words you hear and see all the time. Chances are you have repeated and supported the message, and that is a beautiful thing. It is wise to not settle and everyone seems to celebrate the idea of not settling. If I post on social media "never settle" it will get a huge number of likes and people cosigning on the post. However, when I look around, I still see people settling. I still see women entertaining men who are not worth their time. I still see you in situations where you do not belong. I still see women dragging things out hoping for change, hoping to pull "better" out of a situation you know better is not going to come from. You are settling.

Why?

It makes me question ... *do we really understand why we should not settle?*

Maybe that is the problem.

We can say it all day long but if we are still engaging in it, then we are missing the mark somewhere. We are not connecting with the principle and the premise. It sounds good coming out of our mouths, but are we really embracing it within our spirit? Ask yourself, am I really about this "non-settling" life? Am I really serious about holding strong to that, or am I just speaking it?

I understand the struggle.

There are many factors at play. So much can happen in your life that makes you begin to believe that maybe settling is not that bad of an idea.

You Believe There is Nothing Better

It is a very common perception. You are dealing with a guy and think (pardon my language), "why leave this a**hole to go deal with another a**hole? I might as well deal with the one I already know." It feeds into the idea that you won't find better. Settling becomes tempting and comfortable when you're holding on to this negative perception.

You Are Tired of The Dating Process

I mean, let's be real, it is 2017 and dating is not getting easier. I am aware of this. However, I do believe that with the right tools and approach, you can conquer the obstacles you face in the dating process. Still, I get it. I get that it is hard to deal with and continue on, specifically when it takes what is relative to you as a long or a good amount of time. The process starts to wear you down and you do not want to deal with it.

Again, I get it.

Your Clock is Ticking

The clock ticking is relative because many women don't believe there is a particular age that signifies a "clock"; however, I have heard women in their early 20s talk about it, the same as a woman in her 30s or mid-40s. It all depends on the person and where they believe they should be at that point in their life. Whatever the timeframe or age limit, a lot of women grew up knowing when they wanted to be married and have children. You have set a certain standard, so now when you reach that personal measuring stick, you start to feel the pressure, as well as a bit discouraged and weary. All of these factors start to contribute to your willingness to settle.

Outside Pressure

I grew up with three sisters, one being my twin. I know what outside pressure looks like. I completely understand it. I have seen the pressure put on my sisters to get married and have kids, as well as the pressure put on myself as a man. It is no different.

Still, I get it.

I have seen what women deal with and how insensitive some people can be. Parents, friends, and loves ones wondering why you have not found a man yet, why you have no children, and what is holding you up; as if you are purposely taking longer than you anticipated. They dump all this pressure and these expectations on you, it is unfair.

Here is what happens. In an attempt to make them happy, or shut them up, it forces you into the mindset of settling and accepting the next man who comes along and seems good enough to be with, just to get them out of your ear.

With all that happening (and there is probably more that I missed), I empathize with why, even when you know your worth and embrace your value, it can still occur. I am sure there is a point in your life where you settled, or maybe it is your current situation, but do not beat yourself up or be ashamed about it. I want you to learn and really grasp that as we move forward, settling can no longer be an option and here is why.

#1 – You Will End Up Back at Square One

What do I mean by that?

Quite often, women meet men who appear "good on paper." Despite the red flags and the issues that are clear, they move forward believing they can push through. He is "good enough," even though they know, deep inside (that intuition), that he is not the one. They have decided to settle, they move forward, eventually marry the man who is "good enough," and now things really hit the fan. They realize they are in a relationship that makes them unhappy and struggle to understand why it is not the way they desire. Well, part of them understands why, but they fight it.

They fight it with the hope they can turn it around, try to make right the bad decision they knew was doomed from the beginning. They want to believe they can keep going because they have invested so much, but they are dragging along unhappy and miserable, all because they settled. Eventually, that person will leave. The man will leave, or the relationship will mutually dissolve and what happens then—back at square one.

#2 – Settling is Only a Temporary Fix

Sure, at times temporary could be three, five, ten, or even fifteen years, but I tell you what. There is an expiration date. You may argue that there is an expiration date on real love; however, I do not buy that and neither should you. Even so, at least those who do not settle will be happy until that time comes. It is pointless to accept temporary when it will lead to more issues and heartache. Settling affects your emotional, mental, physical and spiritual health. It deteriorates your overall quality of life because you feel boxed in and that is not going to work for you.

#3 – You Will Never Find Real Happiness

When you are with someone you who you are not happy with, you will always feel a void. There will be emptiness, a feeling of something missing in the relationship. That is no way to live. If you were to have private conversations with some of your friends, your mother, your aunts, and maybe even your grandmother, those who you sense were in similar situations, they can attest to how unhappy, empty, and lonely it felt being in that relationship or marriage for X amount of years. One of the worst positions to be in is to be with someone and still feel lonely.

This happens when you settle.

There will be a void.

You cannot escape it. You cannot run from it and as long as you are there, you will deal with it. The best example I can give is the person who is at a job they hate. Sure, they are there and it gives them a paycheck. They drag along with it, but they are unhappy, miserable, and feel like something is missing. They want out. It feels like a constant prison and they wish they could break free. That is no way to live and it is definitely not the way that God wants you to live. That situation must change because it does not glorify God.

Settling does not give God glory.

God is not in the business of giving you lackluster relationships. He is not in the business of giving you mediocrity. He does not specialize in having you walk around unhappy and miserable over something HE gave you.

No, that is unacceptable.

He wants to give you greatness, something amazing. Why? Because when someone looks at you, at your relationship, and wonders how you got that, or how you are so blessed, you need to be able to say, *God gave that to me. I am blessed because I listened to God and my relationship is blessed because I let God guide me to it.*

When you can testify to what He has done, you are able to impact other people and make them say, *I want what she's having* and they will know the only way to get it is through God.

He would never want you to settle.

If we think of God as a corporation and He is concerned about His brand, you entering relationships with men who do not belong in your life makes God's brand look bad. They do not speak to the truth of what He can do for you; therefore, He would not want that for you. It is a misrepresentation.

❋ ❋ ❋ ❋

Despite all the reasons I have given you not to settle, you may still be tempted at times. Here is how to counteract that.

When you begin to assume there is nothing better, remember, God always has your best interest in mind. There is no myth in that and if you honestly believe He will shortchange you, then there is a deeper issue that needs to be addressed. You have to believe and have faith that since He only wants what is best for you, there will always be better. When I say *better*, it is not in the context of never being satisfied, or constantly moving from person to person. It is knowing He will provide a man who is perfect for you. However, you have to hold strong to that belief and be patient for when that time comes.

If you have become tired of the dating process, stop wasting your time when you date. It is quite simple. Part of the reason you are tired is because you drag out dead end situations with men you should not entertain for so long. It does not take several months or years to figure out he is not the one. You knew after the first date, honestly, you may have known after the first phone call.

Why continue the situation?

When you do that, you develop what I call "dating fatigue." You are so worn out, even when an amazing man comes next, you do not have the energy to embrace him properly. You cannot deal with the situation anymore, so you shut down from dwelling in all that nonsense.

We are all going to experience bad situations and come across bad people. However, you have to hold yourself accountable for situations you entertain far longer than you should. This is where listening to and talking to God becomes essential, as I mentioned previously. Ask Him if you should even entertain this man. Your intuition is just as essential because it tells you when he is not the one and it is time to go. The situation will not magically turn itself around. It is not going to work, move on. Doing this will help prevent you from becoming so worn down with the dating process.

Worried about your clock ticking; then stop setting yourself up with a specific age to accomplish certain things. Place your focus on doing what God wants you to do and trust in His timing. I am aware of the biological aspect regarding pregnancy and the age when it begins to become more difficult, and eventually unsafe to even make the attempt. This topic alone is delicate; however, many of you may not be facing this yet. The more you become antsy and focus on time, the less focus you place on what you should be doing which would accelerate the process of accomplishing your goals. You may get there sooner than you think, if you keep your eye on the prize. If you have approached the time when it gets a bit uncertain, I do not have a quick and simple answer, but I encourage you to pray. I have seen women accomplish childbirth at ages they did not believe it would work.

Each situation is different.

Whether it is having babies or being married, do not put unnecessary pressure on yourself. Focus on what you need to do to reach the finish line.

Lastly, if you are dealing with outside pressure, I could easily tell you to go around and slap everyone, tell them to shut up and leave you alone; however, that is not going to fix anything or give you the peace you need.

I want you to know that you have to be more transparent and honest when people bring up the subject. Let them know how it makes you feel when they continue to badger you. Do not just shut down when they start going in your ear, particularly when it is a parent or someone close to you. Do not let them ramble on and just suck it up, despite how it makes you feel. You need to communicate that it is getting under your skin, so they understand the negative impact it has on you with the constant pressure and badgering.

It is important that you express yourself in a positive and loving manner. They need to understand that they have to fall back. Also, when they ask why you are still single, give an honest answer (*Need help?* visit www.thereasonwhyimsingle.com). When you give a BS answer, you only open the door for them to keep pushing because they sense the BS. They will rattle of, "oh, that does not make any sense," "no, that can't be it," and now they want to push harder, dig further—be honest. *I'm still working on some things,* be honest. *I haven't healed from my past,* be honest. *You know what, I have someone in my life but I'm a little scared of the situation,* be honest. Transparency will help you. Although I cannot guarantee every person will stop, I am confident they will at least slow down.

One more time, you cannot settle.

It is unacceptable.

I do not care if you put sticky notes all over your house, in your car, your purse, on your shoes, but you must always remind yourself that settling is not an option, then embrace it. Remember the consequences of settling. When you make the choice to do so, you rob yourself of the greatness God has for you.

Period.

Do not cheat yourself out of that.

You will get it. Stick to it, put in the work, stay on track, and listen to what God wants you to do. When you adhere to the directions, everything will fall in place and settling will never be an option again.

Trait #4

Trait #4

He Wants a Helpmate,
Not a Playmate

B oys always want to play, while men are ready
to work. Boys look for playmates, while men
desire a helpmate.

Do you see where I am going with this?

The man God has for you is not all about the
games and child's play. He is focused and has a grasp
on what he wants to accomplish in his life and in a
relationship. Lies, unwillingness to commit,
disrespect, and other negative behaviors are not
signs of a man who is serious about being with you.

The man for you does not look at you to be his
crutch, he does not use you. He wants to work with
you, build with you, love you, and pour into you.
You need to be aware of the signs from men who

only look to play. Too many of you, your friends and family members constantly fall into these traps. The red flags are there. You either see and ignore them, or miss them altogether. You overlook the traits and characteristics that tell you whether a man is serious or playing games.

A common issue women experience is the man who is unsure of what he wants. He does not know if he is ready for a relationship, or where he wants things to go.

Let's just go with the flow. Let's not stress things or overanalyze…

It is the most popular phrase men use and if you have been told this, more than likely, he is playing games. He is feeding you BS and to be honest, he is not that confused. He knows what he wants, but he cannot tell you that because he knows he will not get it.

For instance, you meet a man and, quite frankly, he wants to have sex but he will say he wants to have *fun*. He is looking for a no pressure situation where he can enjoy himself at his convenience, everyone is happy, no one is complaining, and he is free to do as he pleases.

But he cannot tell you that.

No matter how many women say *if a man just wants to have sex, just say it and maybe he'll get it,* there is a one percent chance of it actually happening. Of course I am exaggerating a bit; however, in ninety-nine percent of those situations, he is not going to get it.

You are going to shut it down.

Why?

Most women are not looking for that type of relationship. When you do entertain it, more than likely, it is because you have become fatigued with relationships, or you are looking for something convenient and easy due to not healing from previous disappointments. Most times it is not as convenient as you would like, but you want it because you are scared to put yourself out there and be vulnerable. You look for a safer route to companionship.

It is your in between.

You avoid a real relationship because you do not want the pain and disappointment you believe comes with it, so allow yourself to accept "fun," easy, and convenient. Even when you think it is OK, the impact is different when a man is straightforward about his true intentions. When he says to you, *I don't see you as anything more than someone to "kick it" with,* that becomes a harder pill to swallow.

When you say it, when you tell him you see him as nothing more than someone to kick it with, even if he likes you and wants more, you are comfortable with it because it gives you a false sense of control. However, when he is that straightforward, it does not sit well with you. Despite what women have claimed, most men realize when it comes to casual sex and situations of "convenience," being straightforward will not get the result they are looking for in most situations, so what is the alternative?

They lie.

I am not validating the lie or excusing it in any shape or form. However, I guarantee many have tried the straightforward approach and were shut down. Men know they have a better chance of getting what they want by being indirect and suggesting going with "the flow." They will feed you whatever is necessary to continue the situation and drag it along.

Whenever a man wants to "go with the flow," just be his friend. Do not get romantically tied up with a man who does not know what he wants. When he figures it out, he can try again and you two can discuss how to move forward. When you get caught up in that type of situation, it is a recipe for disaster. Accepting the lack of clarity and direction only allows him to remain vague and drag out the situation even longer. It is not impossible for it to change; however, it is extremely unlikely.

When you make decisions, think about what is in your best interest, what is realistic. God does not want you to be romantically tied to a man who is not committed to you, tied to a man who does not see you as his wife or does not want to make you his wife. Why would He want you to entertain a situation like that?

He would not.

The man who does not know what he wants should not be entertained.

Stop Waiting for Him to Be Ready

Many of you may believe that you should wait around until he is ready, be available when he finally "wakes up" and decides he is ready for a commitment. I have spoken to so many women who have this logic and their perception is:

> *He's not there yet but I'm going to stay in his life. I'll show him the good thing that I am and make sure that when he finally comes to a place, when he finally evolves and matures enough to settle down, he will choose me as the woman to do it with.*

That is a horrible approach.

First off, you are not a consolation prize. When a man finally gets to a place where he is done running around and is ready to take the woman who has been there serious, this does not mean he is *in love* with you. It does not mean he desires to be with you, please you, or pour into you. He chose you by default and I promise I am not making this up. I have had men tell me, verbatim, that they chose their woman by default.

While in the barbershop, a man told me he chose his WIFE, the woman he married, simply because **she was the one who was around**, she was the one that **stuck by him**. But guess what? He is not really in love with her. Lo and behold, it is no surprise, they are having issues. It is no surprise that he is contemplating leaving. You do not want him to choose you because you happen to be there when he decided to wake up.

Second, it is not likely for him to just wake up one day and want it. It is a gradual progression, something he has thought about and may very well think about even when he is with you. But again, as I mentioned previously, his whole "I don't know what I want" or "I'm not ready" spiel is just a disguise for I do not see **YOU** as the one. Again this is not to hurt your feelings, it is to help you understand that you do not belong there. And to be honest, there is nothing wrong with him not seeing you as the "one" because *he is* not the one for you.

All you need to do is search deep within yourself, go to God, examine the red flags, and address all the issues to come to a clear conclusion that he is not the guy for you and you are better off walking away.

Do not fall into the trap of waiting until he is ready. Many times the woman who waits ends up being the one who wakes up one day and watches him leave to go be with someone else. He goes and marries some other woman. He tells you he is not ready for marriage, tells you he is not ready for a relationship, then three months later…BOOM!

He is engaged.

Clearly being ready was not the issue, he just did not choose you.

Again, for some of you, I know this hurts to hear and I understand, but it is necessary. It is the kind of medicine you need. It tastes really bad, but it is good for you in the end. You will feel so much better after you digest it, accept it, and move forward. Do not get caught up in the idea of waiting until he is ready.

Do Not Let Mixed Signals Distract You

The next issue is mixed signals.

A lot of men confuse the hell out of you and it makes no sense. They say, *I don't want a girlfriend*, but behave like a boyfriend. They say, *I don't want commitment* but want to regulate who you talk to or who you entertain—it gets downright confusing. They want to cuddle and do all this sweet stuff, but when you ask where this is going, then he says, "whoa, slow up, you're moving too fast! What are you doing?"

Yes, this is confusing, but guess what?

An inconsistent action is a consistent answer ...

And the answer is, he is not serious. He is not ready or willing to be the man you need.

As we discussed in Chapter 2, there is a difference between the person who makes a real effort but makes mistakes at times, and the person who has a recurring issue. When it is continuous, that is a problem. Does he show you effort? What are his words and do they line up with his actions? Even though actions speak louder than words, in this case you can get confused. Oftentimes, his actions may say he wants to be in your life, or wants you as his girl, but his words say no.

The actions and words must be aligned.

When the actions and words do not line up, there is a problem. A lie is being told somewhere, or an issue is not being addressed. One way or another, it needs to be investigated and should not be ignored. When he says you are not his girl, he does not see you as his girlfriend, does not **want** a girlfriend, then does the opposite, the minute you assume he is supposed to be with you, he will come back and say, *I told you I didn't want a girlfriend.*

An inconsistent action is a consistent answer.

The answer is, he is not serious. He is not ready to be what you need. If he was, the consistency would be clear. He would put in the effort, ensure his words and actions lined up, and everything would make sense. All this confusion he creates is because he is either playing a game or there is an issue he has not addressed. Either way, it is something you should not entertain.

It is even more important for you to address the issue because it can easily be a matter of miscommunication or misunderstanding. In the same instance, I am aware that when you try to confront the issue he may dance around it, flip the script to make it about you, what you did not do, or what you did wrong. He will make claims that you are questioning and pressuring him, which backs you into a corner and is ultimately a distraction from the fact he STILL did not answer your question. He gave you no clarity; the issue is still an unsolved mystery.

This all leads to the same conclusion — he is not serious. He is not ready to be in a real, genuine relationship, and there is no need to entertain it any further.

The man God has for you is looking for a helpmate, not a playmate. He is not trying to play games with you. The man who is "God-approved" wants to work with you. He has built himself up to this point and now he wants to build greater things with you. The last thing he wants to do is play you, confuse you, or create nonsense in your life. He is only interested in making you feel more secure about him.

The guy who is serious about you wants you to feel at peace. When you ask him questions he will provide the answers because he wants you to feel safe with him. He wants to show you that he is nothing like those other guys. He wants you to feel confident that he is different and genuine about his intentions with you.

Always know that boys will bring the confusion and chaos, but the man who is serious about you wants to provide clarity and peace. So if necessary, go make yourself a sign that reads: **NO BOYS. NO GAMES. JUST MEN.** Put it on a t-shirt! You can have it. I won't sue you if I see any of you wearing it.

NO BOYS. NO GAMES. JUST MEN.

But make sure you adhere to it and follow it. Do not just speak about it, be about it. Understand that you need someone who is serious. Be open, ready, and willing to put in the work on your end.

Do not get me wrong, we are focusing on the things you need to see in him, but always be mindful of the energy you bring to the table. When you come correct, he has no excuse but to do the same. If he can't come correct, then he needs to go home.

Plain and simple.

Side note: **Do not be an emotional manipulator. If you do not want a man to play with your emotions, do not play with his.**

As of late I've found physical attraction is no longer enough. I need genuine connection. I need to undress the layers of a soul…passion remains the fire, but now intimacy strikes the match, and friendship has become the fuel.

– Beau Tapin

Trait #5

Trait #5

You Will Experience a Genuine Connection, Not Just Chemistry

A 32-year-old woman named Michelle reached her breaking point.

She was frustrated with relationships, believing all the men she met were only after sex. She decided to give up on dating and focus on her career. Before she took that step, she prayed one last time and asked God to finally bless her with the man for her. She believes she is a good woman and deserves to receive a good man.

Two days later, she attended a networking event and met a handsome, put together man exactly her style at about 6'1", strong frame, and a nice smile. They spoke while there and got along well. They exchanged numbers and Michelle went home a happy woman. She was excited, praised God, and believed he might be "the one."

Time progressed and they graduated from dating to a relationship. During this time, she spoke to me about it, along with the potential for it to turn into marriage. I was happy for her; however, I could not help but notice the vibe was not right. I asked more questions and it became clear that although they got along well, there was not a genuine connection. They liked what the other brought to the table; however, they did not enjoy sitting and eating there together.

Think about that.

They were content with hype and surface benefits of the relationship, but take that away and there was not much else happening.

Unfortunately, the relationship eventually dissolved and never made it to marriage. He was not the man God had for her. The proof was in their lack of a genuine connection. Without it, a relationship will not have long term success and you can be assured he is not the man for you.

You will meet a lot of men who will catch your eye, and just as many you would talk to and like. There may even be instances where you believe you love this man, and that may be true; however, you will not experience a deep and genuine connection with every, single one. Such a connection is rare to experience more than once in a lifetime; although, there are exceptions to the rule.

Having a genuine connection with someone is a special experience. It is like two spirits recognizing their counterpart. This does not happen with most people you meet, which is why a special connection is a strong indicator, and a necessary foundation, to recognize that this is the man God sent to you.

Connection vs Chemistry

Now do not confuse connection with chemistry. When I speak to people they will claim to have a "great connection." I will ask what they mean by this and they follow up with stating getting along, liking the same things, or sharing common interests and passions. All of which are great; however, that does not mean there is a deep and genuine connection. Most times, it is just part of the chemistry between two people.

To give more clarity, chemistry accounts for the ability to get along with each other. It is two people happily coexisting with one another. Chemistry is the foundation of a connection, it sets the tone for people to dive deeper, although this may not always happen. When there is a deep and genuine connection, those two people develop a bond. They enjoy each other as they are, and it goes beyond common and shared interests. With a deep and genuine connection, it allows two people to be comfortable with vulnerability. You accept their layers and enjoy simply being in their space. It is easy to unpack who you are with them because there is a mutual acceptance.

This is huge.

You want to be sure the relationship goes deeper than, "we get along." Think about the long-term. If you are not spending extended periods of quality time with a person, chemistry can fool you. This does not mean you need to live with a person; however, there needs to be time spent getting to know one another. You need to talk, open up, share the deeper parts of you. Without it, you will not discover who they are. Although you may not completely know a person, you want to gain a more in depth understanding of them. Getting along with and liking someone, being able to hang out with them only touches the surface—that is chemistry. You want to go beyond that, which can only happen when there is a genuine connection. **Bottom line:** do not confuse chemistry with connection.

Now, how do you determine if the connection is there?

Be Yourself

Many people begin dating, enter relationships, and even marry while holding on to a façade; portraying who they believe they need to be, rather than who they are.

I speak to a lot of women who have "played the role" they thought was necessary, regardless of whether or not it resonated with them. They believed this was the only way to get the man they wanted.

And they got him.

They married and years into the marriage, they are looking at themselves in the mirror, wondering who the hell they are, what happened to them, and who the man is that they are lying next to.

Reality smacks you in the face and you realize the relationship is a mess.

Do not get caught up in who you think you should be. There may be parts of you that need to evolve or improve and that is OK. Embracing this and allowing it to happen is good and healthy for a relationship. However, when those parts do not connect with who you truly are, you will not be able to sustain them and eventually your true colors will show.

Furthermore, you do not want to fake enjoying parts of him. We know it is best to wait for sex until marriage; however, some of you may have crossed that line or considered it. I am using this example because it has a huge impact on relationships and marriages.

There are more stories than I can count where women who sleep with men are not satisfied, then act as if everything is great because they want to get to the altar. You have held on to or chose to believe that this is what you want, so you act as if you enjoy the sex, as if you are content with his long hours at work, or OK with the lack of time he gives you. You deal with all the aspects you are not satisfied with and soon enough, you cannot keep it up anymore and the entire relationship blows up in your face.

This is an example of lacking connection.

You were not happy there.

When there is a connection, you are at peace with this person. You enjoy them, you are comfortable being with them, and you want to be in their presence. You are content with them, even with their imperfections. With a genuine connection, there is no need to fake it. Everything is natural.

Being yourself is key because if you are not yourself, then who will they connect to?

I always say you cannot create, nor destroy, a genuine connection. There are people who have not seen each other in ten, twenty, or thirty years and when they get together, it is as if nothing has changed, the feelings resurface. Those genuine feelings cannot be faked or denied. You can fake the chemistry, you can tolerate behaviors and people. You can choose to ignore it and move along; however, if the connection is not there, it just is not.

But you can also run away from a connection.

When you are afraid to be vulnerable, you put up walls and hold back which can cause the man to do the same. You may believe the wall is there to protect and guard your heart, but as I mentioned in *God Where Is My Boaz*, you are actually just blocking your blessings. Biblically speaking, guarding your heart is specific to protecting it from fear, anger, negative energy, and others things that will corrupt or darken it. That is what you want to guard your heart from, not a genuine connection which makes you feel vulnerable.

You cannot go into potential relationships, holding back who you are. You will sabotage the situation. You hurt your chances of being able to embrace the connection you may have with the guy who is for you, and in the same instance, fool yourself into thinking it is OK to be with a guy who does not belong in your life.

Take a Road Trip Together

I am not talking about a two-hour drive, I am talking six hours or more. A drive where the two of you can do nothing else but sit and talk—no distractions. There is no other choice but to get to know each other.

How does the conversation flow? Is it fluid? Are you learning more about one another? Do you feel a stronger, more intimate connection, or are you ready to kick him out the car before you get to the third hour? If you cannot do a road trip, then spend an extended period of time together with no distractions and really see if you two enjoy each other. This will help you to determine if there is a genuine connection.

A lot of people are in relationships, right now, where they seem happy. Everything appears great and wonderful; however, they would not last an hour alone in a car together. They need a distraction because they do not really like each other in that way. They are caught up in the surface hype, the fantasy, the image of what they want things to be, and what they want to believe they are; however, they are not dealing with reality.

Do not set yourself up like that.

You have to make time to sit, talk and vibe together. You do not have to do it every week or every day, but if you cannot make it happen then I am sorry to tell you, it is going to be a problem. Without true quality time, you might be able to tolerate the relationship for awhile and push forward simply for the sake of having a relationship. The fact remains, you are setting yourself up for disaster. People who have genuine connections do not struggle with this. They can meet and speak for hours and it is nothing to them.

Some of you may be thinking, *I spoke to this guy on the phone for hours and it still didn't work out.* Using the phone as a measuring stick can be risky because you do not know what distractions are on their end, or what they are using to help move things along. It may be easy to mask the connection in the first couple of conversations; however, at some point, you are forced to go in depth if you intend to keep the conversation going, otherwise, it is just small talk.

When you go more in depth, it begins to draw out the information. You begin to see if you two truly connect, share the same values, and want the same things in life. This is how you know if there is genuine a connection. Do not ignore this. You cannot overlook these conversations and expect to gain a true depiction and understanding of who you are dealing with, and if they are best for you.

Trust Your Intuition

Any of you who follow me on social media, have read *God Where Is My Boaz*, or any of my work, know I am big on intuition. Your intuition is a gift, a blessing. It is rare for a woman's intuition to be wrong, and most times I want to say it is never wrong; however, to be fair, I will say it is *rarely* ever wrong.

It is a matter of being willing to listen because you know when he is not it. You know when the connection is not there and you know when something deeper is missing. It may scare you, or you may try to rationalize why it is not there. There are various reasons why you choose to ignore your intuition; however, it is not that you do not know, you simply struggle to embrace it. Your intuition is there for a reason, it is a blessing, and you have to refrain from the continuous pattern of ignoring it. It is dangerous to do so.

Think about it, when is your intuition wrong? Why ignore what you felt on the first date, or the first week talking to the guy? You know he is not the one, yet you spend the next few weeks, months, or years being with someone, then see it end. A lot of times, you see it end the same way your intuition told you. There is no point in doing that or dragging things along.

You do not need to "give things a chance," it is not necessary. When you give the unnecessary a chance you waste time. When you recognize that you do not belong there, yet you continue, you waste time. The risk of further damage occurs, which keeps you farther off the path God wants you to follow. This does not mean you cannot still get your blessings, or get back on the right track, but it does delay the process.

We have all done it, We are human.

We can pray, hear it and sometimes still move forward against what God has told us—it happens. However, embracing your intuition will help you break that pattern. You have to be willing to listen. No one has to tell you that the connection is not there with a guy, you will know. No one has to tell you that it *is* there. You will know it, you will feel it.

But are you willing to be honest with yourself and embrace it?

Bottom line, you cannot and should not ignore the lack of a connection. In the end, it is one of the necessary steps in building the foundation of a successful relationship.

We talk about high divorce rates, how love and relationships are not the same, people do not value commitment, etc. Then we pile on explanations such as the generation of today, people being raised poorly, the sex, finances, and a host of other reasons. All of this stems from a lack of connection. When you have a genuine connection, you want to work through things together. However, when the connection is not there, and the money is not right, or the sex is off, now you are forced to face the reality that you never liked the person and never wanted to deal with them in the first place. You may not say it, but part of you thinks it.

If there is no genuine connection, there is not enough desire and love for each other to want to overcome these obstacles, to want to persevere. Even in situations where people stay together, despite that lack, they are not working past those issues. They move things along and let things pile up until one day it completely explodes, and they cannot keep it together anymore.

There are other ramifications that can occur from this disconnect which leads to a extremely unhealthy household. Despite believing staying together is best, the disconnect can negatively affect the children. It may have happened in some of your lives. You may have grown up in a household where your parents (married or single) created a false and unhealthy perception of love and relationships. An unhealthy environment due to broken relationships and people who had no connection trying to deal with one another.

It does not work.

It is dangerous and I do not want you to move forward ignoring it. That is not what God wants. He knows a deep and genuine connection is necessary for success.

As I said earlier in the chapter, a connection is like two spirits recognizing their counterpart. God wants you to be with your counterpart. He wants you to be with the person you are truly aligned with and be able to walk the path He has designed for you both. That is not going to happen in a relationship where there is no real connection.

Be mindful of this.

Keep your eyes open, do not ignore your intuition. Know that you have to truly to connect this person. You have to like who they are and that starts with being yourself. Get to know who you are, love who you are, show the world. Then, the man that is for you, who truly loves you, will embrace that person.

Talk to God

How to Talk to God

The Most Popular Prayer Women Pray

I had a client once who we will call "Patricia." Patricia came to me because she was struggling with relationships.

She was frustrated and could not understand why she did not have greater success in that area, despite her belief of being a great catch. Overall, Patricia was successful and accomplished, but when it came to love and men, things always fell apart. So my question, always, at some point in the session is *did you pray and ask God should you be dealing with these men?* I am not going to summarize her response because I want you to see the dialogue between her and I, as well as think about how you would respond when asked the same question. Can you see any similarities?

Patricia: "Yeah, I prayed."

Me: *What exactly did you pray?*

My follow-up question is important because we may pray; however, we need to know exactly what it is we are praying for. It is crucial that we come to God with the right questions and approach, seeking the correct guidance in the situation.

> Patricia: "I prayed and told God if this is not for me, <u>please remove this man from my life</u>."

Now, the reason why I highlight that specific prayer is because it is probably one of the most popular prayers a woman of God prays—*Lord, remove him if he is not for me.*

> Patricia: "That is what happened, I prayed that and a couple weeks later he was gone. And every time I pray that prayer, that guy ends up leaving. So, you know, that is what I do, that is how I pray to God."

Let me pause right here and make something crystal clear to you right now, that is the **wrong prayer**. Sorry to burst your bubble and disappoint you. I will say it again, that is the WRONG. PRAYER. As popular as it is and as comforting as it may be, simply telling God to take this person away and let it be done is the wrong request.

Here is why, you ask God to remove this person if they are not for you. Then, you go into a wait and see mode, observing the situation, waiting to see what happens next. You may see nothing wrong with it, believing you are allowing things to happen in "God's time"; however, when you take a wait and see approach, while you are dating or getting to know someone, you hold back. You do not show much interest, take initiative, make a mutual effort to grow and nurture the relationship, or discover if there is a deep and genuine connection.

Now your wall is up because that is essentially what you do when you hold back. You restrict your ability to love and receive love, stunt the growth, and kill the potential of that relationship. While you are thinking this man disappeared or fell back from your life because God moved him, more than likely it is because you pushed him away. It is easier for a man to chase lust, than it is for him to chase love.

What do I mean by that?

When we lust after someone, those reservations, the resistance, the walls are not going to faze that man much. Why? He is locked in on the desire, his selfishness to fulfill whatever conquest he has in mind. He has a goal he is trying to achieve and your resistance will not stop that. However, when he is truly into you and real feelings are involved, now your resistance gives him pause. It makes him scared, feel insecure, and question if you are really into him.

As much as you may not want to believe it, men get played too. They may not get played as much as women, but way more than you realize. In light of this, a lot of men approach things cautiously and when you start to hold back, you have thrown up a red flag. Eventually, he will walk away because he does not want to deal with it, or it hurts too much to try to push past it.

This is not to say that the man was not removed based on your request to God, or that every man who has walked away was a result of being pushed away. Nor does the man's unwillingness to let you go mean he is the man for you. I just want you to understand that this approach of asking God to remove certain men from your life can lead you to pushing away the man who you can potentially have a great relationship with. Again, if he has genuine interest, he is more sensitive to what is occurring in the situation. This will cause him to hold back because you are. If you want to expose a man's true intentions, then you have to be genuine about yours. How can you find out if his feelings are real, when you are not being real with how you feel?

It does not work like that.

Simply relying on God to remove a man is not the way to do it. The better approach is to ask God *should* you be dealing with this man, is he for you, and *how should* you proceed? The key words I am using focuses on you asking for direction on how to navigate the situation. This goes back to what I said before, you have to come to God ready to listen. You are not there to only make a petition or vent. You come to Him to ask for direction, listen, and then be obedient to what you are told.

Some of you may feel as if trying to listen to God is too complicated, or may not be sure how to decipher if you are listening to yourself or what God is trying to tell you. I get it. There is much to address regarding hearing God; however, your intuition is your first guide. As a woman of God, it is your spirit that is trying to reach you, talk to you, and get your attention. It is rare to find a woman who can say her intuition was wrong.

Plain and simple.

It is not a matter of you not being able to hear, it is more about you getting comfortable with what you are hearing, even if it is something you do not want to hear. That is usually the reason why directions and instructions are missed. You have to reconsider your approach if you want to ensure you are dealing with the right person.

Another aspect to consider when making sure you hear the right thing is opening yourself up to receive the answer. Here is an analogy: when we pray, it is like you are a child taking a test. Your parent is a few rooms down the hall and you are screaming the question to your parents, hoping to hear the answer because you do not want to get up and go in front of their face to listen. And they are answering you. They are answering your question but you cannot hear them from that distance. You need to get up, go in their room, in front of their face, and then listen.

So guess what?

When you say, I am praying and I am not hearing anything from God, well, maybe it is because you need to get up, move into His room, into His face, and listen. This could mean you need to fast, clear out all the clutter and distractions, pick a time, then find a quiet and peaceful place to pray. Be sure you are calm and not praying in a moment of anxiety, frustration, or anger. From there, you can come to God and draw yourself closer to Him, so that you can hear more clearly because I assure you that you will hear Him. You have to enter prayer in submission, being open and welcome everything He has to say to you, even if it is not what you want to hear. More times than not, we will not like it. However, it is what we need and what is best.

Ultimately, you have to stop asking God to do it for you.

The responsibility is yours.

To be clear, I am no biblical scholar. Although I incorporate God into my message, along with spirituality and prayer, I am not a pastor or the "church-y" guy. I cannot quote scriptures; however,

I have read parts of the Bible and continue to learn more.

What I have noticed is that people of God who have accomplished great things went on great journeys, and had amazing experiences. They were given instructions. It was not a simple process. God is not just going to drop the blessing in your lap. You can't just chill and hide in the corner while he takes care of everything for you. It was not about them making petitions and God waving some magical wand over them.

No.

It was about them getting specific directions and following it. This led to them to great results because faith without works is dead. What this shows, consistently, is that it's on you to remove the person, take the action, and learn what needs to be done. How will you learn and grow in your faith if you do not take action on your own.

Again, think about the scenario of being a child. If the child has everything done for them, how will they ever learn? How do they grow, become stronger, wiser, and better equipped to handle the next obstacle that life will throw at them? I do not care who you are, life will throw some speed bumps your way, along with some mountains you have to climb. That is just the way it is. When you learn how to take action with God's guidance, you build faith, strength, resilience, and wisdom. You grow, and only then are you able to accomplish more in your life, as well as impact and help the lives of others around you, be it directly or indirectly.

It is important for you to understand your role in the process, along with the actions you must take. This includes all aspects of your life. God cannot coddle you. I would love for it to be easy, we just put in our request and everything is done, but that is just not the way it works. You will be better off once you accept and embrace this approach.

From here on out, I need you to promise that you are not going to pray that prayer again. You will not ask God to remove that person if they are not for you. From now on ask, *Lord, should I remove them? Should I be dealing with them and how do you want me to proceed?* When you ask this, you will find out what you need to do, then you must do it. You will see the greatness of being obedient, getting His direction, and experiencing the blessing that comes along with that journey. Although it may be tough, you will love it in the end and you will see the results.

So, find peace with that.

God is there to hear you and give you an answer. It is what He wants. Being open to hearing Him will only strengthen your relationship and that is a good thing, so let's make that happen. Let's continue with this new approach and continue on with this book.

Trait #6

Trait #6

He Will Love God

*There is no perfect man; therefore,
there is no perfect man of God.*

B ased on our beliefs, we were born into sin, so
we are going to make mistakes. We all have a
process in our lives where we grow, evolve, and
begin to understand how to properly approach life
and anything else we encounter on that path.
Perfection is unrealistic; therefore, there is no
perfect man and there is no perfect man of God.

Many times we place expectations on people
once they have accepted God. It is an assumption
that now they are supposed to get it all right. They
are not allowed to sin, have faults, or struggle. The
minute we view it, we take it as proof that they are

not serious, not truly a believer, a hypocrite, or just playing games.

We want to discredit them.

Too many believers are too quick to judge and look down upon someone for their lack of perfection. We know people are not perfect, yet somehow we forget that when mistakes are made.

I want you to understand, the man God has for you will love God but this does not mean he will be perfect. His love of God is what needs to be in place for you to be able to accept him into your life. Without that foundation, not only will he make mistakes, that man will not be aligned with you. He'll be someone who will struggle understanding how he needs to pour into you, treat you, and cherish you as the blessing that God gave him. His love of God needs to be there, but this does not always lead to perfect behavior.

So how do you know if he is a man of God? What criteria can you use to assess a man and his genuine love for God?

The first step is to understand the difference between *a man who loves God and struggles with his flesh*, versus *a man who loves his flesh and struggles with embracing God.*

The man who loves God and struggles with his flesh is no different than you. He may embrace prayer and the understanding that God wants him to walk a greater path, as well as be better in the way that he approaches such things as who he is to be as a man.

He gives credit to God, he is aware and can humble himself in the fact that he cannot accomplish anything without the power that God gave him, the love that God showed him, or the guidance that God provided him.

However, he is human, just as you.

Oftentimes, there are certain behaviors that reflect his past or everyday life struggles where he may fall off track, or at least be tempted. Behaviors adverse to his walk may appear and you might be quick to say he's not serious. However, when he can acknowledge his errors, understand the need to find ways to improve, and not reject facing God on the issue, then you know He is trying to walk the right path. He may not attend church as much as you want, worship how you think he should, or even be as passionate when he comes to God in reverence and prayer. These instances are where you two may differ; however, it doesn't necessarily define him as a man who isn't genuine about God.

On the flip side, the man who is in love with his flesh but struggles to embrace God is a man who does not respect your walk. He is not able to encourage your growth in God, or his own. Some of these men don't particularly reject with their words what they need to do, because they put on a convincing act. They're in church just like you, can quote scriptures and can speak in a way a Godly man would, but their behaviors are consistently distant from a man of God's path, and they aren't willing to address their issues.

It is one thing to struggle here and there, it is another to continuously behave inconsistent to what God wants them to do and attempt to get you to engage in the same behaviors. They try to pull you away and remain unwilling to consult God about the matter. A man like this is much more in love with his flesh, than he is with God.

Neither are perfect, nor will they always get it right, but there is a clear difference between the two. The Bible says, *judge a person by the fruit of their spirit.*

Even if he acts the part, what is he producing? It is the same as I mentioned in Chapter 4, do his actions and his words align?

Again, you have to be in tune with your own spirit and be willing to pray for that discernment, so you can see that this guy is not for real and he is not who he proclaims himself to be. This leads to the part of being *unequally yoked*.

A lot of people have different perceptions on what it means to be equally yoked. Again, I am no biblical scholar and I do not have a perfect understanding of every concept from the Bible or from God; however, what I believe is that you and the other person have to be on the same accord. Do not confuse this with doing things the same. We may not all worship the same, know all scriptures like the next person, or be as strong in reciting prayer, but we are both willing to head on the path towards God and put Him first. That has to be in place.

This is essential because many people try to overlook or downplay the importance of being equally yoked and sharing the same values.

Problems will occur when you start a relationship with someone who is unequally yoked. It may be

OK for you in the beginning. It may not be until after the first few months or years before you start to see a clash. How intense you two clash, will depend on how strong your walk is with God compared to how off it is with theirs. However, in time, it will become a problem.

I will never forget one couple who were both believers, one was Methodist and the other Jehovah's Witnesses. They had a difference of opinion when it came to their child receiving medical treatment. If their child was in a car accident and needed a blood transfusion, the person who was Jehovah's Witnesses did not believe in or accept blood transfusions, while the one who was Methodist did. To someone on the outside looking in, that may not be a big deal. What are the chances of that happening?

Thing is it is not even about the chance of it happening, it is about these two people not being able to be on the same page when a certain issue arises. This is when everything would fall apart.

Here's a simpler example. Let's say you get with someone who believes in God but he doesn't care for church and is a passive believer so to speak. You on the other hand are very serious about church and your faith. Everything seems good, until an issue comes up where you two disagree. You feel strongly about it and say, *hey, we need to pray about it* and he responds, *pray about it? Pray about it for what? We don't need to pray*. His logic tells him certain steps are needed in order to solve the problem, and to him praying isn't one of those steps.

This is where you two will clash and everything will begin to spiral.

Nothing big may have occurred prior; possibly small things here and there that began to irk, poke, and pull you in the wrong direction. However, this clash can turn into a lack of trust, feeling like your beliefs are devalued, and a host of other issues. You may choose to ignore them; however, there will come a time where you can't anymore and it'll become a problem.

So being equally yoked means that you and your man have to be in agreement about how to handle life situations, your values, the goals you pursue together, and how you view relationships. Even in a non-religious context, it would still apply. But when you are unequally yoked, there is no togetherness, you are going to work apart, clash and conflict with how to handle life.

Reminder:
No man is perfect.
He will love God but he will not be perfect.

It is important to keep this in mind because you may meet a man who is still "in his process." He is in a growth stage with God and is taking the time to evolve and shed some of the old ways that are no longer in his best interest, as well as become more intimate in his relationship with Him.

There is no perfect way to journey through this stage. For various reasons you may not recognize that he is in it. You may have skipped this process or it could be different from your own, so you may not understand or respect where he is.

For example, I will never forget the time I was invited to do a speaking event at someone's house. The organizer had a group of women over and one, who is pretty much the most respected woman in her church, approached me after I spoke (I separated the conversation as I did before):

The Woman: I'm fifty-one years old, never been married, and really want to but I don't know what to do at this point.

Me: *In all those years, have you ever been proposed to?*

The Woman: Yes. I've been proposed to three times.

It gets better...

Me: *What happened? Did you decline all of them?*

The Woman: Yes.

Me: *Why?*

The Woman: Oh, because they weren't at the level spiritually where they needed to be.

Me: *Oh. So you decided for yourself that they weren't good enough spiritually, or at the level you felt they should be, meaning matching yours so to speak, but did you ever stop and ask God?*

The Woman: No.

Moral of the story: just because you have evolved to a certain level does not mean a man who does not match it should be automatically dismissed.

To be clear, I am not saying to get with him now in his current phase. This is why praying and asking God, and getting His consultation is so important. It may be a situation where this guy needs some time. Chances are, if he needs some time, there are some things you need to work on and then you two will come back together. But if you completely dismiss it without going to God because he does not pass YOUR test, you could be shooting yourself in the foot. His love of God may not reflect your same behaviors with regard to how he worships, prays, reads the Bible and so on; however, this does not mean his relationship with God is not as good as yours, or that yours is better.

You have to be mindful of completely using your own logic and metrics to determine who is the best fit for you. That is why the name of this chapter is *He Will Love God*, not "he will be the perfect Christian," not "he will do XYZ." He will love God and from there you have to pray and ask if this is the man for you and if you should be with him. For all we know, there may be a friendship that needs to occur first before things can go further. Do not dismiss it, or shut it down. Be open to what needs to happen and you can only know that by going to God.

Now with that said, I am going to reiterate some things we discussed in Chapter 3 about building man. You are not here to save this man. More specifically, **you are not here to save him while attempting to enter into a romantic relationship.**

Remember, being friends is the acceptable option while he is in his stage of growth. It may be your friendship that helps him get closer to God. You may encourage him, be the light that leads him in the right direction; however, none of this needs to happen within the dynamic of a romantic relationship.

When the wrong man realizes this is all you want, as long as he plays the role, he may play along to continue to reap the benefits of a relationship with you. Even those who are not serious about God can attempt to play the role without truly having to meet the standards necessary to be in a relationship with you. As I mentioned in Chapter 3, this is where you get distracted, lose focus, and divert off the prize that is your path and purpose. You become so caught up in saving this man that you do not recognize that it is pulling you further away from God and damaging you in the process.

That is not your job.

Again, always go to God. Always ask Him and be open to the role He wants you to play. However, I am pretty sure, within this context, it is not going to be a romantic one. Know that if a man has not reached a point where he loves God, then it is not time to be with him, or align yourself with him in that manner. You have to be patient and know that this is not guy for you, or this is not the time. Your season in his life may just be a temporary one, or you may not belong there at all.

Keep your eyes open.

Make sure your love and focus for God does not waver or becomes impacted by your desire for a man. The man who loves God will not pull you from that path. He will encourage you to remain on it, grow stronger in it, and for you two to grow together in becoming and being in the position that God wants for you both in life.

Trait #7

Trait #7

He Will Want All Your Love, Not Just a Piece

A *whole man wants a whole woman.*

Let that marinate for a second.

As a matter of fact, let me repeat it for you, *a whole man wants a whole woman.* You desire a man that is well rounded and well put together, so what do you think he wants? You want a man who can be open, honest, and give you all of his love. What do you think he will want? You would love to have a man who does not come with a heap load of baggage and issues.

So, how about yours?

Have you addressed and corrected them?

The type of man you truly desire, this amazing man that God has for you, will come with a higher standard of living in the way that he carries himself. Things that may get by with unhealthy men, the ones who are not together or not walking in their purpose are not going to fly with the man that God has for you. It is going to be a different ball game and you have to hold yourself to the same qualities and standards you want in a man, as well as embrace the qualities he looks for in a woman.

Many of you may believe you already have it together and are doing what you are supposed to, but is it fact? Have you made sure? Have you dug deep within yourself, looked in the mirror and made sure you are where you need to be as the woman God created? If not, it can throw EVERYTHING off and even stop that man from presenting himself.

There are a lot factors at play when dealing with the man God has for you.

Some believe, *if it's meant to be, then it will be*; however, that is not the case. People make bad decisions, block their blessings, or walk an alternate path that was not laid out by God. While on that path, they miss what He has for them. It can happen and you must be mindful of this. The man that is for you will want ALL of you, not "the broken down" version who isn't embracing healing and growth.

Another thing to consider is that this guy will be more in tune to feelings. I did not specify yours or his because it will encompass both.

Again, it is a lot easier to chase lust instead of love.

The man who is for you has a genuine desire for you, he considers you as someone he wants to spend the rest of his life with, he will pay more attention to what you do and do not do. He will struggle more when he senses you holding back, or may question your interest when he sees you are not really giving yourself to him. He will be afraid because to love someone means to be vulnerable. As women, you know this. So when he is vulnerable and open and does not see you putting in equal effort, or at least meeting him halfway, he will pause. The negative thoughts will start and give him reason to fall back. This is an absolute truth when it comes to the man who is genuinely interested in you.

On the other hand, the man who wants to have fun views you as someone to kick it with, or a temporary girlfriend (yes there are men who think like this). He only wants you around for the benefits you provide. Holding back or the willingness to love is not of his concern; however, one who is genuinely into you and loves you will notice the wall you have built immediately. He will be more concerned and have reason to question, as well as pause things. As he is more in tune to you, he will pick up on it quicker than the average guy, so when you hold back, have your wall up, shield your feelings, and refrain from clarity, specifically when he asks what is going on, it creates an environment of doubt and insecurity.

Again, it is vital that you are mindful of the energy you put out and the impact of you holding back. I am emphasizing the effects of this behavior because it will get dismissed and you will see it as not a big deal; however, there are issues that can arise.

Just because this man is the one God has for you, does not mean he is going to scale or withstand your walls or get through all your issues and problems.

He cannot heal you.

He will never be able to get through your walls because he is human, just like you and I. If the two of you meet when each of you are broken, it will escalate. There are three key issues you create when you hold back.

Insecurity

If a man does not feel secure, loved, and respected, he will not only begin to question you, he may respond negatively to the block you have created. This is not to excuse any negative behavior or the ways he handles the situation; however, it may prompt such behaviors as being overprotective, being clingy, screening everything you do, and other ways to gain control. Honestly, insecurity is nothing more than an uncertainty and a lack of control. Remember, some of these men are entering relationships with baggage, and more often than not, he was not the man you were supposed to deal with anyway. Or, at the very least, it was not time because he still needed to address and heal those issues.

Also, secrecy always breeds insecurity. Yes, a lot of men tend to be secretive all the time, which is why there are a lot of insecure women in relationships. Their partners lack clarity and openness, with little to no honesty or transparency. The unsaid does not go unnoticed, so if you do not speak on what is ailing you, it will make some men feel uneasy.

Holding back creates insecurity.

Cause a Man to Walk Away

Do not think for one second, that just because this man is of God, he will stick around, tough it out, and jump through hoops and hurdles just to get through your emotional blockade—it is just not true.

I have sat down with a lot of people individually, and with potential couples who I knew were for each other, as well as had a deep and genuine connection. However, because of their past, outside circumstances, and not connecting with what God wanted them to do, the relationship did not proceed. There were many regrets and they later understood what they needed to do differently. Although, at that time, they handled things the wrong way.

He may have his own fears and even if he has worked past some things, he may not want to deal with the resistance. Be honest about whether or not you are being open, inviting, and receptive to his efforts. Do you validate holding back with "guarding your heart"?

Remember what we covered in Chapter 5. Guarding your heart pertains to protecting it from fear, anger and anxiety; it does not mean you shield yourself from being open and receptive to the man who is genuinely into you. If you continue to use this as an excuse, it will only hurt you in the end. Like the old saying goes, *don't cut your nose to spite your face.*

Are You Really Listening to God?

I can tell you right now, when God wants you to do something or has someone for you and wants you to proceed, none of it is with the idea of holding back. Be clear that when you do this you are operating out of fear, not faith, which means you are not approaching the relationship the way God wants.

I get it.

It is scary and your feelings are valid. I am not judging you for being afraid and I do not want you to beat yourself up over it either, especially if you have done this before or are experiencing it currently. However, what I need you to understand is this is not OK and it goes against what God wants you to do. The only reason to run is because God told you it is time to go.

When you attempt to move forward while holding back in fear, you miss the opportunity to see the full potential of the relationship. You have to move past any hesitation. Either you are going to do it, or not. If you have already prayed and God gave you to the answer to move forward, then you need to do it with full force. You will have to open up and be vulnerable, this is what is required. Without it, you will sell yourself short.

On many occasions, people have shared with me this piece of advice: *a woman should be with a man who loves her more than she loves him.*

If you agree with this, then I sincerely want you to know that this is a misguided mindset to have. Not to be harsh, but quite frankly, it's horrible advice. It is also a setup for disaster every single time. The idea of quantifying who loves who more indicates there is a problem from the start.

Again, the man God has for you will share a deep and genuine connection. If you speak to anyone who has experienced this, they will tell you there is no way to compare who loves who more. They are into each other, period. The connection is too strong for you or anyone to determine whose love is greater for the other. If there is a distinction, the love between you and the man you are with is imbalanced and that is not where you need to be.

Love should be reciprocated. If you want to have a great love, you have to set the bar. You cannot enter a relationship waiting to see what they are going to do, or if they will put forth all the effort. Because this particular man is sensitive and in tune emotionally, he will realize you are playing chess with his heart, not being receptive, and showing the effort he needs. Eventually, he will think you are not serious, get tired and walk away. In turn, you will think he was not serious because he did not stick around and deal with your mess.

No.

He left because you kept holding back and it happens every single day. Do not believe you should look for the man who loves you more. As we discussed, there needs to be alignment, as well as a deep and genuine connection. In order for you determine the alignment and connection, you have to be open and vulnerable, as well as embrace the love you have for this person. All of this goes back to the root of addressing your issues. Have you resolved any lingering fears? Have you healed from your past and completed the work within, for you to receive, accept, and nurture the great relationship God has for you?

A whole man will want a whole woman.

You have to work on being whole. It is not about finding a man who completes you, it is about completing yourself and receiving the man who complements you, as you complement him in return. That is the relationship that will flourish and become something amazing.

Be willing to give all of yourself and if you are not ready, then you know there is work to be done. Do not be afraid of it. We all have room for improvement and things we need to work on in life. We all have to embrace learning, growing, evolving and healing because we have all been hurt. We have all been damaged at some point. But there are those who work, resolve, and arise from it greater than ever, and those who dwell in it.

Make sure you are not the one who is dwelling in it.

Conclusion

Ultimately, I hope after reading this book you have gained a lot of insight, some peace, and clarity on the things you need to be aware of while you prepare yourself to receive the man God has for you, as well as evaluate if he is in fact, the right man.

If you go back and read, *God Where Is My Boaz*, it is one of the key premises I present—prepare and position yourself. You want to be sure that is something you are working on as you move along this journey because you are no longer "waiting" for Boaz. You are in the process of receiving the man God has for you.

While in this process, you are doing your part and becoming your best self. Regardless of what happens romantically in your life, becoming your best self is most important. It is important with regard to being in alignment with where God wants you to be, as well as receiving all the opportunities and blessings He has for you.

It is not just about a man, there is a bigger picture here.

It all comes together when you get right yourself and find your purpose. When you love yourself, heal, get rid of past hurts, disappointments, and flush that negative energy out of your system. You become the woman you were created to be and that is a beautiful thing.

However, let's get back to the man that you are going to receive along this journey.

I want you to know that it is possible, in some scenarios, for you to meet that guy and he is the one, but it is not time yet—right guy, wrong time. I have heard people say if it is the wrong time then he cannot be the guy, and that is not true. Many people cross paths with each other at a time when they are not ready, or it is not time for them to get together romantically. We assume somehow that because we meet someone and we have feelings, that we now have to move forward into a romantic relationship.

No, not necessarily.

God may want a process to occur before that time comes. For all you know, you meeting him is so that you can see what is coming, so that you can see the blessing is there. But, there is still some work to be done, and it is not just work on the man's end. Some of you may have met that guy and he was not ready or he had some things he needed to get in order, and to be honest, that happens. However, if it is not time for you both this means there is stuff that you need to work on too.

Never think so highly of yourself that you believe there is no room for improvement. Humble yourself before God, understand that you have to open yourself up to whatever growth and lessons He wants you to learn, so that you can be better equipped for that relationship. Because if you do not get your ducks in a row, I guarantee when you two do come together, things will fall apart.

That is not what I want for you.

I want you to experience that amazing, successful, long-lasting relationship that everyone dreams of. You can have this for yourself. Again, sometimes it is the right person, wrong time and that is why praying and talking to God is so significant. It is critical in knowing how to handle things.

Here is a quick example:

I have a client who met a man a year ago. She really liked him. They spoke and he said to her, straight up, "I am not ready yet, I need to get some things in order. I'm still working on my relationship with God, it's just not time." After he expressed that to her, he fell back to where he stopped calling and interacting. As a result, she was hurt and upset by his actions, and understandably so. She instantly believes the guy is not for her, leaves him alone, and kills it.

A year later, the guy pops back up and she is still holding on to the anger and resentment in how he handled things. Even though, when you really look at it, he was trying to be responsible and honest about where he was and was not trying to play games; yet, she was still angry and resentful. When he pops back up, she is rejecting the idea of even finding out why he is back in her life. However, I encouraged her to pray and ask God what He wants her to do in this situation. She prayed and it led to God telling her to respond to him and she did.

Long story short, they ended up reconnecting and she saw the growth that occurred in him. They really hit it off and everything clicked. Although she started to get scared again, she continued to pray and God told her to move forward with him and this process. That story is still being written and it is moving along nicely.

I give you that example as a reminder to always be willing to pray and ask God. Do not allow your emotions to get in the way. Do not allow your fear to stop you. Understand that just because it was not time then, does not mean it cannot be time now.

I want you know to that you can have the relationship of your dreams. There *is* a man that God wants for you. You have to believe that you can receive it, which is the first step in this entire process—believing.

Believe and trust in God, then be willing to learn what steps you need to take. Be aware and keep your eyes open to what was discussed in this book on how to recognize and understand who and what you are dealing with.

But none of this ever overrides God's direct word to you in prayer. That is what I always want to encourage you to do. It is what I always believe is most important for you and if you embrace this, you will always remain on the right track, and you will always get what you deserve in life and more.

About The Author

S tephan Labossiere is a man on a mission, and that mission is to make relationships happier and more fulfilling.

As a certified relationship coach, a speaker and author, Stephan seizes every opportunity to help both men and women overcome the challenges that hinder their relationships. From understanding the opposite sex, to navigating the paths and avoiding the pitfalls of relationships and self-growth. Stephan's relationship advice and insight helps countless individuals achieve an authentically amazing life. Stephan empowers millions to take charge of the difficult situations standing in the way of the life and love they seek and to make impactful changes on a daily basis.

Dedicated to helping, and devoted to keeping it real. Stephan's straightforward, yet compassionate delivery style, attracts a versatile clientele including; notable celebrities, civic and social organizations, academic institutions, singles, and couples alike, who can and are ready to handle the truth!

Seen, heard and chronicled in national and international media outlets including; the Tom Joyner Morning Show, The Examiner, ABC, Huffington Post Live, and GQ to name a few. Stephan is highly sought-after because he is able to dispel the myths of relationship breakdowns and obstacles--platonic, romantic, and otherwise with fervor and finesse.

To borrow a phrase coined by an individual who attended one of his speaking engagements, "he's definitely the relationship guy, all relationships, all the time."

With an international following of singles and couples alike, the name Stephan Labossiere is synonymous with breaking down relationship barriers, pushing past common facades, and exposing the truth. It is this understanding of REAL relationships that he brings to everyone he encounters.

Other Books & Resources

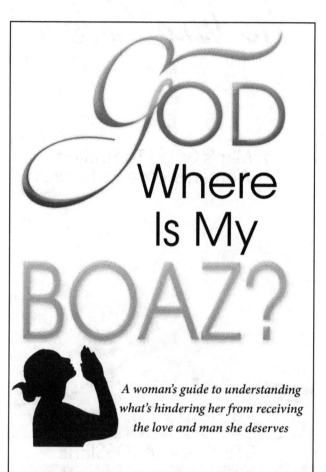

www.GodWhereIsMyBoaz.com

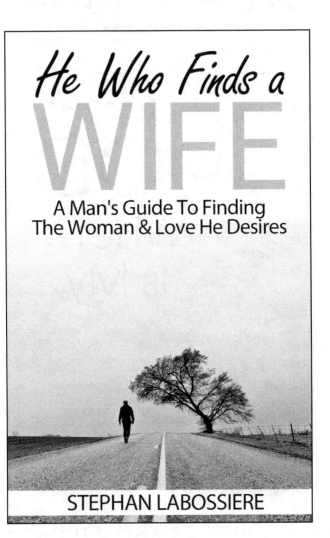

www.HeWhoFinds.com

WHY MEN OVERLOOK
THE GOOD GIRLS
MP3 Audio Teleseminar

STEPHAN LABOSSIERE

www.WhatAboutTheGoodGirls.com

Resources and more can be found at
stephanspeaks.com/products

You can also follow me on
Twitter & Instagram: **@StephanSpeaks**
or find me on Facebook under
"Stephan Speaks Relationships"

CPSIA information can be obtained
at www.ICGtesting.com
Printed in the USA
FSHW01n0208270618